the
Spanish
Travelmate

compiled by
Lexus
with
Alicia de Benito Harland
and
Mike Harland

LEXUS

First published 2004 by Lexus Ltd
60 Brook Street, Glasgow G40 2AB, Scotland
www.lexusforlanguages.co.uk
Maps drawn by András Bereznay
Typeset by Elfreda Crehan
Series editor: Peter Terrell

ISBN 978-1-61894-340-8

Printed in the USA

Your Travelmate

gives you one single easy-to-use A to Z list of words and phrases to help you communicate in Spanish.

Built into this list are:

• travel tips (✈) with facts and figures which provide valuable information

• Spanish words you'll see on signs and notices
• typical replies to some of the things you might want to say
• language notes giving you basic information about speaking the language
• a menu reader on pages 82-85

There are maps of Spain and the Spanish islands on pages 153-158. Numbers and the Spanish alphabet are on pages 159-160.

Speaking Spanish

Your Travelmate also tells you how to pronounce Spanish. Just read the pronunciation guides given in square brackets as though they were English and you will communicate – although you might not sound exactly like a native speaker.

If no pronunciation is given this is because the Spanish word itself can be spoken more or less as though it were English and a pronunciation guide would add nothing new.

In a few cases where the Spanish translation is in fact an English word then this translation is put in quotes.

Sometimes only a part of a word or phrase needs a pronunciation guide.

Stress

Letters in blue show which part of a word to stress, or to give more weight to, when speaking Spanish. Getting the stress right is particularly important.

In Spanish itself, whenever you see a letter with an acute accent above it (like **allá** or **está** or **avión**), this accent shows which part of the word is stressed.

Some special points about the pronunciation system used to represent Spanish:

ah	like the a in f**a**ther
air	like the air sound in h**air**
ay	like the ay in p**ay**
eh	like the e sound in w**e**t
g, gh	like the g in **g**o
H	from the back of the throat, like the ch in the way Scots pronounce lo**ch**
I	like the i in h**i**
oo	like the oo in b**oo**t
ow	like the ow in c**ow**
th	like the th in **th**eatre

Men and women speaking

When you see an entry with a slash like:

bored: I'm bored estoy aburrido/a
[...aboor**ee**do/a]

the Spanish given after the slash is the form to be used by female speakers. So a man would say:

I'm bored estoy aburrido

and a woman would say:

I'm bored estoy aburrida

When two translations are given, as in:

these estos/estas

the first is for masculine nouns (with **un**, **el** or **los**) and the second for feminine nouns (with **una**, **la** or **las**).

Language backup

To find out more about Lexus and Lexus Translations or to comment on this book you can go on-line to www.lexusforlanguages.co.uk.

A [ah]

a, an un; una [oon, **oo**na]

abierto open

about: is he about? ¿está por aquí? [...ak**ee**]

  about 15 unos quince [**oo**noss k**ee**ntheh]

  about 2 o'clock sobre las dos [s**o**-breh...]

above por encima [...enth**ee**ma]

abroad en el extranjero [...estranн**eh**-ro]

absolutely! ¡desde luego! [d**e**zdeh lw**eh**-go]

accelerator el acelerador [atheh-lerad**o**r]

accept aceptar [athept**a**r]

accident el accidente [aktheed**e**nteh]

  there's been an accident ha habido un accidente [ah ab**ee**do oon...]

> ✈ Remember to take an E111 form (from the Post Office). Dial 112 for any kind of emergency – ambulance, fire, police etc.

accurate ex**a**cto

across: across the street al **o**tro lado de la calle [...l**a**hdo...ka-yeh]

adaptor un adaptad**o**r

address la dirección [deerekth-y**o**n]

  will you give me your address? ¿me quiere dar su dirección? [meh kee-**eh**-reh...]

adjust ajustar [aноost**a**r]

admission la entrada [entr**a**hda]

advance: can we book in advance? ¿se pueden hacer las reservas *por adelantado*? [seh pw**eh**den ath**air**...adelant**a**hdo]

advert un anuncio [an**oo**n-thee-o]

afraid: I'm afraid so me temo que sí [me t**eh**-mo keh...]

  I'm afraid not me temo que no

after después [despw**e**ss]

after 9 después de las 9
after you usted primero [oos**teh** pree-m**eh**-ro]
afternoon la tarde [t**a**rdeh]
  in the afternoon por la tarde
  this afternoon esta tarde
aftershave el 'aftershave'
again otra vez [**o**-tra beth]
against contra
age la edad [eh-d**a**]
  under age menor de edad [meh-**nor**…]
  it takes ages se tarda mucho [seh t**a**rda
  m**oo**tcho]
ago: a week ago *hace* una semana [**a**teh **oo**na
  sem**ah**na]
  it wasn't long ago no hace mucho tiempo
  […m**oo**tcho tee-**e**mpo]
  how long ago was that? ¿cuánto tiempo hace
  de eso? [kw**a**nto…deh **eh**-so]
agree: I agree estoy de acuerdo […deh akw**air**do]
  it doesn't agree with me no me sienta bien
  [no meh see-**e**nta bee-**e**n]
agua potable **drinking water**
air el aire [**ı**-reh]
  by air en avión [ab-y**o**n]
air-conditioning: with air-conditioning con aire
  acondicionado […**ı**-reh akondeeth-yon**ah**do]
air hostess la azafata [athaf**a**ta]
airmail: by airmail por avión […ab-y**o**n]
airport el aeropuerto [ah-airo-pw**air**to]
airport bus el autobús del aeropuerto [owto-
  b**oo**ss del ah-airo-pw**air**to]
aisle seat un asiento de pasillo [ass-y**e**nto deh pa-
  s**ee**yo]
alarm clock un despertad**o**r
alcohol el alcohol [alko-**o**l]
  is it alcoholic? ¿tiene alcohol? [tee-**e**h-neh…]
alive: is he still alive? ¿*vive* todavía? [b**ee**-beh

todab**ee**-ah]

all todo [t**o**do]
  all night toda la noche [t**o**da la n**o**tcheh]
  all the flights todos los vuelos
  that's all eso es todo
  that's all wrong está todo mal
  thank you – not at all gracias – de nada [grath-
  yass – deh n**ah**-da]

all right de acuerdo [deh akw**air**do]
  it's all right está bien [...bee-**en**]
  I'm all right estoy bien

allergic: I'm allergic to... soy alérgico a... [al**air**-
  нeeko]

allowed: is it allowed? ¿está permitido? [...
  pairmeet**ee**do]
  allow me permítame [pair-m**ee**ta-meh]

almost casi [k**ah**-see]

alone solo
  did you come here alone? ¿ha venido solo/a?
  [ah...]
  leave me alone déjeme en paz [d**eh**нemeh em
  path]

alquiler de coches car hire
already ya
also también [tamb-y**en**]
although aunque [**o**wng-keh]
alto halt
altogether del todo
  what does that make altogether? ¿cuánto es
  en total? [kw**a**nto...tot**a**l]
always siempre [see-**em**-preh]
am¹ *(in the morning)* de la mañana [...man-y**ah**-na]

  ✈ In timetables the 24-hour system is used.

am² *go to* **be**
ambulance una ambulancia [amboolanthee-a]
  get an ambulance! ¡llame a una ambulancia!

[y**a**h-meh...]

✈ Dial 061 for an ambulance or 112 in any case of emergency.

America Am**é**rica
American *(adjective)* americ**a**no
  (man) un norteameric**a**no [norteh-]
  (woman) una norteameric**a**na
among entre [**e**ntreh]
amp: a 13 amp fuse un fusible de trece
  amperios [foo-s**ee**-bleh deh tr**e**htheh amp**e**h-ree-
  oss]
anchor el ancla
and y [ee]
andén platform
angry enfadado [enfad**ah**do]
  I'm very angry (about it) estoy muy enfadado
  por ello [...mwee...**e**h-yo]
ankle el tobillo [tob**ee**-yo]
anniversary: it's our anniversary es nuestro
  aniversario [...nw**e**stro...]
annoy: he's annoying me me está molestando
  [meh...]
  it's very annoying es muy molesto [...mwee...]
anorak un anor**a**k
another: can we have another room? ¿puede
  d**a**rnos *otra* habitación? [pw**e**hdeh...abee-tath-
  y**o**n]
  another beer, please por fav**o**r, otra cerveza
  [...thair-b**e**h-tha]
answer la respuesta [resp**we**sta]
  what was his answer? ¿qué respondió? [keh
  respond-y**o**]
  there was no answer no hubo respuesta
  [...**oo**bo...]
antibiotics unos antibióticos [antee-bee-**o**tee-koss]
antifreeze el anticongelante [antee-konнel**a**nteh]

any: have you got any bananas/butter? ¿tiene plátanos/mantequilla? [tee-**eh**-neh...]
  I haven't got any no tengo [...t**e**ng-go]
anybody cualquiera [kwal-kee-**eh**-ra]
  we don't know anybody here no conocemos a *nadie* aquí [no konoth**eh**-moss ah n**ah**d-yeh ak**ee**]
  can anybody help? ¿alguien puede ayudar? [al-ghee-en pw**eh**deh ah-yoo-d**a**r]
anything algo
  I don't want anything no quiero nada [...kee-**eh**-ro n**ah**-da...]
aparcamiento car park
apology: please accept my apologies por fav**o**r, acepte mis disculpas [...ath**e**pteh meess deess-k**oo**lpass]
appendicitis la apendicitis [apendee-th**ee**-teess]
appetite el apetito [apeh-t**ee**to]
  I've lost my appetite he perdido el apetito [eh pair-d**ee**do...]
apple una manzana [man-th**ah**-na]
apple pie una tarta de manzana [...deh man-th**ah**-na]
appointment: can I make an appointment? quería pedir hora [ker**ee**-a ped**ee**r **o**ra]
apricot un albaricoque [albareek**o**keh]
April abril [abr**ee**l]
aqualung una botella de oxígeno [bot-**eh**-ya deh ox-**ee**-Heno]
are *go to* **be**
area (*neighbourhood*) la zona [th**o**na]
area code el prefijo [pref**ee**-Ho]

✈ Whether you're in Spain or calling from abroad you have to include the zero of the area code.

---

arm el brazo [br**ah**tho]

around *go to* **about**

arrange: will you arrange it? ¿lo arreglará usted? [...oost**eh**]

arrest (*verb*) detener [deh-ten**air**]

arrival la llegada [yeh-g**ah**-da]

arrive llegar [yeh-g**ar**]

  we only arrived yesterday llegamos tan sólo ayer [yeh-g**ah**-moss...ah-y**air**]

art el arte [**art**eh]

art gallery un museo de pintura [moo-s**eh**-o...]

  (*private*) una galería de arte [...deh **art**eh]

arthritis la artritis [ar-tr**ee**-teess]

artificial artificial [arteefeeth-y**al**]

artist un pintor [peen-t**or**]

  (*woman*) una pintora

as: as quickly as you can lo más de prisa que pueda [lo mass deh pr**ee**-sa keh pw**eh**-da]

  as much as you can tanto como pueda

  as you like como quieras [...kee-**eh**-rass]

ascensor lift

aseos toilets

ashore: to go ashore desembarc**ar**

ashtray un cenicero [thenee-th**eh**-ro]

ask pregunt**ar**

  could you ask him to...? ¿podría pedirle que...? [pod-r**ee**-a ped**eer**-leh keh]

  that's not what I asked for no había pedido eso [no ab**ee**-a ped**ee**do **eh**-so]

asleep: he's still asleep todavía está durmiendo [todab**ee**-a esta door-mee-endo]

asparagus un espárrago

aspirin una aspirina [aspeer**ee**na]

assistant (*in shop*) el dependiente [deh-pendee-**enteh**]

  (*woman*) la dependienta [-dee-**en**ta]

asthma el asma [**a**zma]

at: at the café en el café

at one o'clock a la una
at Cristina's en casa de Cristina
atención al tren beware of trains
attitude una actitud [akteet**oo**]
attractive: I think you're very attractive (*to man/woman*) me pareces muy guapo/a [meh par**eh**-thess mwee gw**a**-po/a]
aubergine una berenjena [beren-H**eh**-na]
August ag**o**sto
aunt: my aunt mi tía [mee t**ee**-a]
Australia Australia [ows-tr**a**h-lee-a]
Australian (*adjective*) australiano [-y**a**h-no]
Austria Austria [**ow**stree-a]
authorities las autoridades [ow-toree-d**ah**-dess]
automatic automático [owto-]
autopista motorway
autoservicio self-service
autovía dual carriageway
autumn: in the autumn en otoño […o-t**o**n-yo]
away: is it far away from here? ¿está muy lejos de aquí? […mwee l**eh**-Hoss deh ak**ee**]
 go away! ¡lárguese! [l**a**rgheh-seh]
awful terrible [ter**ee**-bleh]
axle el eje [**eh**-Heh]

B [beh]

B (bajo) ground floor
baby un bebé [beh-b**eh**]
 we'd like a baby-sitter quisiéramos una baby-sitter [keess-y**eh**-ramoss…]
back (*of body*) la espalda
 I've got a bad back padezco de dol**o**r de espalda [pad**e**th-ko…]
 at the back por detrás
 I'll be right back estaré de vuelta pronto [estar**eh** deh bw**e**lta…]

is he back? ¿ha vuelto ya? [ah bw**e**lto…]
can I have my money back? ¿me puede
devolver el importe? [meh pw**eh**deh deh-
bolb**air**…-teh]
I go back tomorrow me vuelvo mañana [meh
bw**e**lbo…]
backpacker un mochilero [motchee-l**eh**ro]
   (female) una mochilera
bacon bacon
   bacon and eggs huevos con bacon [w**eh**-
   boss…]
bad malo [m**ah**-lo]
   it's not bad no está mal
   too bad! ¡qué le vamos a hacer! [keh leh b**ah**-
   moss ath**air**]
bag una bolsa
   (suitcase) una maleta [mal**eh**ta]
   (handbag) un bolso
baggage el equipaje [ekee-p**ah**-нeh]
baker's la panadería [-**ee**-a]
balcony un balcón
   a room with a balcony una habitación con
   balcón [abee-tath-y**o**n…]
bald calvo
ball *(football etc)* una pelota
ball-point (pen) un bolígrafo
banana un plátano
band *(musical)* la orquesta [ork**e**sta]
   (pop) un grupo
bandage una venda
   could you change the bandage? ¿quiere
   cambiar el vendaje? [kee-**eh**-reh kambee-**a**r el
   bend**ah**-нeh]
bank *(for money)* el banco

✈ Opening hours: 8am-2pm, Mon-Fri; some
city centre banks open Sat for a few hours.

bank holiday *go to* **public holidays**
bar el bar
  in the bar en el bar

➤ Most bars have table service and you pay
  when you leave.

YOU MAY HEAR
¿qué desea usted? *what will you have?*

---

barber's una peluquería de caballeros [pelookeh-
  ree-a deh kaba-**yeh**-ross]
bargain: it's a real bargain es una verdadera
  ganga [...bairda-d**eh**-ra g**a**ng-ga...]
barmaid la camarera [kamar**eh**-ra]
barman el camarero [kamar**eh**-ro]
baseball cap una gorra de béisbol
basket un cesto [th**e**sto]
bath un baño [b**a**n-yo]
  could you give me a bath towel? ¿me podría
  dar una toalla de baño? [meh podr**ee**-a dar **oo**na
  to-**ah**-ya deh...]
bathroom el cuarto de baño [kw**a**rto deh b**a**n-yo]
  we want a room with bathroom queremos
  una habitación con cuarto de baño [keh-r**eh**-
  moss **oo**na abee-tath-y**o**n kon...]
  can I use your bathroom? ¿puedo usar su
  cuarto de baño? [pw**eh**do oos**a**r soo...]
battery una pila [p**ee**la]
  (for car) la batería [bateh-r**ee**-a]
be ser [sair]

There are two Spanish verbs for 'to be': **ser**
and **estar**. **Ser** is used for states which
don't change.
  I am English soy inglés

Estar is used for states which are not
permanent.

he's in his room está en su habitación

ser
I am soy
you are *(familiar)* eres [eh-ress]
you are *(polite)* es
he/she/it is es
we are somos
you are *(familiar plural)* sois [soys]
you are *(polite plural)* son
they are son

estar
I am estoy
you are *(familiar)* estás
you are *(polite)* está
he/she/it is está
we are estamos
you are *(familiar plural)* estáis [estɪs]
you are *(polite plural)* están
they are están

be good sé bueno [seh bweh-no]
don't be lazy no seas vago […seh-ass…]

beach la playa [pla-ya]
  on the beach en la playa
beans unas judías [Hoodee-ass]
  runner beans judías verdes […bair-dess]
  broad beans unas habas [ah-bass]
beautiful precioso [preth-yo-so]
  (view, room, wine) estupendo [estoopendo]
  that was a beautiful meal ha sido una comida
  estupenda [ah seedo oona komeeda estoopenda]
because porque [por-keh]
  because of the weather debido al mal tiempo
  [debeedo…tee-empo]
bed una cama

a single bed una cama individual […
eendeebeedoo**a**l]
a double bed una cama doble […d**o**h-bleh]
 I'm off to bed quiero acostarme [kee-**eh**-ro
akost**a**r-meh]
you haven't changed my bed no me ha
cambiado las sábanas [no meh ah kambee-
ahdo…]
bed and breakfast alojamiento y desayuno [alo-
 нam-y**e**nto ee dessa-y**oo**no]

> ✈ There's no real equivalent to the B&B.

bedroom un dormit**o**rio
bee una abeja [ab**eh**-нa]
beef la carne de vaca [k**a**rneh…]
beer una cerveza [thairb**eh**-tha]
 two beers, please dos cervezas, por fav**o**r

> ✈ If you ask for **una cerveza** you will get **un
> tubo** [t**oo**bo] – 33cl, unless you specify **una
> caña** [kan-ya] which is just under half a pint
> – 25cl. **Cerveza** implies lager-type beer.

before: before breakfast *antes* de desayunar
[**a**n-tess deh dessa-yoo-n**a**r]
 before we leave antes de march**a**rnos
 I haven't been here before nunca había
estado aquí [n**oo**nka ab**ee**-a est**a**hdo ak**ee**]
begin: when does it begin? ¿cuándo empieza?
[kw**a**ndo empee-**eh**-tha]
beginner un/una principiante [preen-theep-
y**a**nteh]
behind detrás
 behind me detrás de mí
Belgium Bélgica [bel**н**eeka]
believe: I don't believe you no le *creo* [no leh
kr**eh**-o]
 I believe you le creo

bell *(in hotel, on door)* el timbre [tee-m-breh]
belong: that belongs to me eso es mío
  who does this belong to? ¿de quién es esto?
  [deh kee-en...]
below abajo [abah-Ho]
  below the knee debajo de la rodilla [debaHo...
  rodeeya]
belt un cinturón [theen-]
bend *(in road)* una curva [koorba]
berries unas bayas [ba-yass]
berth *(on ship)* una litera [leet-eh-ra]
beside junto a [Hoonto ah]
best el mejor [meHor]
  it's the best holiday I've ever had son las
  mejores vacaciones de mi vida [...meHoress
  bakath-yoness deh mee beeda]
better mejor [meHor]
  haven't you got anything better? ¿no tiene
  nada mejor? [no tee-eh-neh...]
  are you feeling better? ¿te sientes mejor? [teh
  see-entess...]
  I'm feeling a lot better me siento mucho
  mejor
between entre [entreh]
beyond más allá [mass ah-ya]
  beyond the mountains más allá de las
  montañas [...montahn-yass]
bicycle una bicicleta [beethee-kleh-ta]
bienvenido welcome
big grande [grandeh]
  a big one uno/una grande
  that's too big eso es demasiado grande [...
  demass-yahdo...]
  it's not big enough no es suficientemente
  grande [...soofeeth-yenteh-menteh...]
  have you got a bigger one? ¿tiene otro más
  grande? [tee-eh-neh...]

bike una bici [b**ee**thee]

bikini un bikini

bill la cuenta [kw**e**nta]
  could I have the bill, please? la cuenta, por favor

bird un pájaro [p**a**-нaro]

birthday el cumpleaños [koompleh-**a**n-yoss]
  happy birthday! ¡feliz cumpleaños! [fel**ee**th…]
  it's my birthday es mi cumpleaños

biscuit una galleta [ga-y**eh**ta]

bit: just a little bit sólo un poquito […pok**ee**to]
  that's a bit too expensive es un poco caro
  a bit of that cake un pedazo de esa tarta [ped**a**h-tho…]
  a big bit un pedazo grande […gr**a**ndeh]

bitter *(taste)* amargo

black negro [n**eh**-gro]

blackout: he's had a blackout se ha desmayado [seh ah dess-ma-y**a**h-do]

blanket una manta

bleach *(for cleaning)* la lejía [leн**ee**-a]

bleed sangrar

bless you! *(after sneeze)* ¡Jesús! [нeh-s**oo**ss]

blind *(cannot see)* ciego [thee-**eh**-go]

blister una ampolla [amp**o**-ya]

blocked *(pipe)* atasc**a**do
  (road) cort**a**do

blonde una rubia [r**oo**b-ya]

blood la sangre [s**a**ngreh]
  his blood group is… su grupo sanguíneo es… [soo gr**oo**po sang-g**ee**n-eh-o…]
  I've got high blood pressure tengo la tensión alta […tenss-y**o**n…]
  he needs a blood transfusion necesita una transfusión [nethess**ee**ta **oo**na transfooss-y**o**n]

bloody: that's bloody good! ¡genial! [нen-y**a**l]
  bloody hell! *(annoyed, amazed)* ¡Dios mío! [d**ee**-

oss…]

blouse una blusa [bl**oo**-sa]

blue azul [ath**ool**]

board: full board pensión completa [penss-y**on** kompl**eh**-ta]

  half board media pensión [m**eh**d-ya…]

boarding pass la tarjeta de embarque [tarH**eh**-ta deh emb**a**rkeh]

boat un barco

  (small) una barca

  when is the next boat to…? ¿cuándo sale el siguiente barco para…? [kw**a**ndo s**a**h-leh…seeg-y**e**nteh…]

body el cuerpo [kw**air**po]

  (corpse) un cadáver [kad**a**bair]

boil: do we have to boil the water? ¿es necesario *hervir* el agua? […nethess**a**r-yo airb**ee**r el **a**hg-wa]

boiled egg un huevo pasado por agua [w**e**h-bo pass-**a**hdo por **a**hg-wa]

bolt el cerrojo [theh-r**o**Ho]

bone un hueso [w**e**h-so]

bonnet *(of car)* el capó

book un libro

  can I book a seat for…? deseo reservar un asiento para… [deh-s**e**h-o reh-sairb**a**r oon ass-y**e**nto…]

  I'd like to book a table for two quisiera reservar una mesa para dos personas [keess-y**eh**-ra…**oo**na m**e**h-sa]

> *YOU MAY THEN HEAR*
> ¿para qué hora? *for what time?*
> ¿a nombre de quién? *and your name is?*

booking office el despacho de billetes […deh bee-y**eh**-tess]

bookshop una librería [leebreh-r**ee**-a]

boot una bota
(of car) el portaequipajes [porta-ekee-paнess]
booze: I had too much booze last night
bebí demasiado anoche [bebee demass-yahdo
anotcheh]
border la frontera [fronteh-ra]
bored: I'm bored estoy aburrido/a [...abooreedo/
a]
boring: it's boring es aburrido [...abooreedo]
born: I was born in... nací en... [nathee...]
go to **date**
borrow: can I borrow...? ¿puede prestarme...?
[pwehdeh prestarmeh]
boss el jefe [нeh-feh]
(woman) la jefa
both los dos [loss doss]
I'll take both of them me llevo los dos [meh
yeh-bo...]
bottle una botella [boteh-ya]
bottle-opener un abrebotellas [ah-breh-boteh-
yass]
bottom *(of person)* el trasero [traseh-ro]
 at the bottom of the hill al fondo de la cuesta
[...kwesta]
bouncer el gorila [goreela]
bowl *(for soup etc)* un cuenco [kwenko]
box una caja [kah-нa]
boy un chico [cheeko]
boyfriend el amigo [ameego]
bra un sostén
bracelet una pulsera [poolseh-rah]
brake el freno [freh-no]
 could you check the brakes? ¿quiere revisarme
los frenos? [kee-eh-reh reh-beesarmeh loss freh-
noss]
 I had to brake suddenly tuve que
frenar bruscamente [toobeh keh freh-nar

brooskam**e**nteh]
he didn't brake no frenó

brandy un coñac [kon-y**a**k]

bread el pan

could we have some bread and butter? ¿nos
pone un poco de pan con mantequilla? [...p**o**-
neh...manteh-k**ee**-ya]

some more bread, please más pan, por fav**o**r

> ✈ Ask for **una barra** (like a fat baguette) at
> the baker's – best eaten the same day.

break *(verb)* romper [romp**air**]

I think I've broken my arm me parece que me
he roto el brazo [meh par**eh**-theh keh meh eh r**o**-
to el br**ah**-tho]

you've broken it lo ha roto usted [lo ah r**o**-to
oost**eh**]

break into: my room has been broken into me
han *desvalijado* la habitación [meh an dess-balee-
н**ah**do la abee-tath-y**o**n]

my car has been broken into me han abierto
el coche [meh an abee-**air**to el k**o**tcheh]

breakable frágil [fr**ah**-нeel]

breakdown una avería [abeh-r**ee**-a]

I've had a breakdown he tenido una avería [eh
ten**ee**do...]

a nervous breakdown una crisis nerviosa
[kr**ee**seess nairbee-**o**sa]

> ✈ Call your insurance company and ask them
> to supply you with list of reciprocal services
> before you go.

breakfast el desayuno [dessa-y**oo**no]

> ✈ Try typical **chocolate con churros** – fritters
> dunked in hot chocolate.

breast el pecho

breathe respirar [respeer**a**r]
 I can't breathe no puedo respirar [no
 pw**eh**do...]
bridge un puente [pw**e**nteh]
briefcase la cartera [kart**eh**-ra]
**brighten up: do you think it'll brighten up
 later?** ¿cree que se despejará? [kr**eh**-eh...keh seh
 despeh-н**a**r**a**]
brilliant *(person)* brillante [bree-y**a**nteh]
 (idea, swimmer) estupendo [-toop**e**ndo]
 brilliant! ¡genial! [н**e**ny**a**l]
bring traer [trah-**air**]
 could you bring it to my hotel? ¿podría
 traérmelo a mi hotel? [podr**ee**-a trah-**air**-meh-lo
 ah mee o-t**e**l]
Britain Gran Bretaña [...bret**ah**n-ya]
British británico
brochure un folleto [fo-y**eh**to]
 have you got any brochures about...? ¿tiene
 algún folleto sobre...? [tee-**eh**-neh alg**oo**n fo-
 y**eh**to s**o**h-breh]
broken roto [r**o**-to]
 it's broken está roto
brooch un broche [br**o**tcheh]
brother: my brother mi hermano [mee air-m**ah**-
 no]
brown marrón
 (tanned) moreno [mor**eh**-no]
browse: can I just browse around? ¿puedo
 echar una ojeada? [pw**eh**do etchar **oo**na o-нeh-
 ah-da]
bruise un carden**a**l
brunette una morena [mor**eh**-na]
brush un cepillo [thep**ee**-yo]
 (painter's) un pincel [peen-th**e**l]
bucket un cubo [k**oo**bo]
buffet un buffet [boof**eh**]

building un edificio [-f**ee**th-yo]
bulb una bombilla [-b**ee**ya]
  the bulb's gone se ha fundido la bombilla [seh
  ah foond**ee**do...]
bull el toro
bull fight una corrida de toros [kor**ee**-da deh...]
bumbag una riñonera [reen-yon**eh**-ra]
bump: he's had a bump on the head se ha
  dado un *golpe* en la cabeza [seh ah d**ah**do oon
  g**o**lpeh en la kab**eh**-tha]
bumper el parachoques [-cho-kess]
bunch of flowers un ramo de flores [r**ah**-mo deh
  fl**o**ress]
bunk una litera [leet**eh**-ra]
bunk beds unas literas [leet**eh**-rass]
buoy una boya [b**o**y-ya]
bureau de change una oficina de cambio [ofee-
  th**ee**na...]
burglar un ladrón
burgle: our flat's been burgled nos han robado
  el piso [noss an rob**ah**do...]

---

they've taken all my money se han llevado
todo mi dinero [seh an yeh-b**ah**do t**o**do mee
deen**eh**-ro]

---

burn: this meat is burnt esta carne está
  quemada [...k**a**rneh...keh-m**ah**-da]
  my arms are burnt me he quemado los brazos
  [meh eh keh-m**ah**do loss br**ah**-thoss]
  **can you give me something for these
  burns?** ¿puede darme algo para estas
  quemaduras? [pw**eh**deh d**a**rmeh...keh-
  mad**oo**rass]
bus el autobús [owto-b**oo**ss]
  which bus is it for...? ¿qué autobús va a ...?
  [keh...]

could you tell me when we get there?
avíseme cuando lleguemos [ab**ee**seh-meh
kw**a**ndo yeh-gh**eh**-moss]

✈ For cheaper travel buy a **bono bus** (book of
tickets) on the bus or in a local tobacconist
or **estanco**; tickets must be punched in the
machine when boarding and are usually
valid for any distance and for one change
of bus (**transbordo**).

business: I'm here on business estoy aquí de
negocios [...ak**ee** deh neg**o**th-yoss]
none of your business! ¡no es asunto suyo!
[...ass**oo**nto s**oo**-yo]
business trip un viaje de negocios [bee-**ah**-Heh
deh neg**o**th-yoss]
bus station la estación de autobuses [estath-y**o**n
deh owto-b**oo**ss-ess]
bus stop la parada del autobús [par**ah**-da del
owto-b**oo**ss]
bust el pecho
busy (streets, bars etc) concurrido [-koor**ee**edo]
(telephone) comunicando [-mooneek**a**ndo]
are you busy? ¿estás ocupado/a?
but pero [p**eh**-ro]
not...but... no...sino... [...s**ee**no]
butcher's la carnicería [karneetheh-r**ee**-a]
butter la mantequilla [manteh-k**ee**-ya]
button un botón
buy: where can I buy...? ¿dónde puedo
comprar...? [dond**eh** pw**eh**do...]
by: I'm here by myself he venido *solo/a* [eh
ben**ee**do...]
are you by yourself? ¿estás solo/a?
can you do it by tomorrow? ¿puede tenerlo
hecho para mañana? [pw**eh**deh ten**ai**rlo **e**tcho...]

by train/car/plane en tren/coche/avión
I parked by the trees aparqué junto a los
árboles [aparkeh ноonto ah loss arboless]
who's it made by? ¿quién lo fabrica? [kee-en lo
fabreeka]
by Picasso de Picasso [deh...]

C [theh]

C hot
c/ street
caballeros gentlemen
cabbage una col
cabin *(on ship)* un camarote [kamaroteh]
cable *(electric)* un cable [kah-bleh]
café una cafetería [kafeh-teh-ree-a]

> ✈ **Cafetería/café/bar** are all roughly
> equivalent: all sell non-alcoholic and
> alcoholic drinks and snacks (**tapas**); open
> all day; children welcome; sometimes
> cheaper to eat or drink at the bar and you
> may be charged more if you sit outside on
> the **terraza**.

caja cash desk
cake una tarta
  (small) un pastel
calculator una calculadora
caliente hot
call: will you call the manager? ¿quiere *llamar* al
director? [kee-eh-reh yamar al deerektor]
what is this called? ¿cómo se llama esto?
[...seh yahma...]
 I'll call back later *(on phone)* volveré a llamar
[bolbeh-reh...]
call box una cabina telefónica [...teh-leh-fonee-ka]
calm tranquilo [trankeeelo]

calm down! tranquilícese [trankee-lee-theh-seh]
cambio de sentido exit here to join opposite carriageway
camcorder una videocámara
camera una máquina de fotos [makeena...]

✈ You won't be allowed to use a flash in most museums and at most monuments.

camp: is there somewhere we can camp? ¿hay algún sitio donde podamos acampar? [ɪ algoon seet-yo dondeh...]
we are on a camping holiday estamos de camping

✈ Camping carnet not essential; camping off-site is no longer allowed in most areas and you will have to ask for permission.

can we camp here? ¿se puede acampar aquí? [seh pwehdeh...akee]
campsite un camping
can¹: a can of beer una lata de cerveza [lah-ta deh...]

✈ Bars usually sell bottled rather than canned drinks.

can²: can I have...? ¿me da...? [meh...]
can you show me...? ¿podría enseñarme...? [pod-ree-a ensen-yar-meh]
I can't... no puedo... [no pwehdo]
I can't swim no sé nadar [...seh...]
he/she can't... no puede... [no pwehdeh]
we can't... no podemos... [no pod-eh-moss]
Canada Canadá
cancel: I want to cancel my booking quiero *anular* mi reserva [kee-eh-ro anoolar mee reh-sairba]
can we cancel dinner for tonight? ¿podríamos

no cenar aquí esta noche? [podr**ee**-amoss no theh-n**a**r ak**ee**...]

candle une vela [b**e**h-la]

can-opener un abrelatas [ah-brehl**a**h-tass]

capsize volcarse [bol-k**a**r-seh]

car un coche [k**o**tcheh]

carafe una garrafa

caravan una carav**a**na

carburettor el carburad**o**r [-boo-]

cards las cartas

  do you play cards? ¿juegas a las cartas? [Hw**e**h-gass...]

care: goodbye, take care adiós, cuídate [... kw**ee**da-teh]

careful: be careful ten cuidado [...kweed**a**hdo]

car-ferry un ferry

car park un aparcamiento [aparkam-y**e**nto]

carpet la alf**o**mbra

  (wall to wall) la moqueta [mok**ch**ta]

carrier bag una bolsa

carrot una zanahoria [thana-**o**ree-a]

carry llevar [yeh-b**a**r]

carving una talla [t**a**-ya]

case *(suitcase)* la maleta [mal**e**h-tah]

cash el dinero [dee-n**e**h-ro]

  I haven't any cash no tengo dinero en efectivo [...efekt**ee**-bo]

  will you cash a cheque for me? ¿podría hacerme efectivo un cheque? [pod-r**ee**-a ath**air**-meh efekt**ee**-bo oon ch**e**h-keh]

  I'll pay cash voy a pagar al contado [... kont**a**hdo]

cash desk la caja [k**a**h-н]

casino el casino

cassette una cassette

cassette player un cassete [kass**e**h-teh]

castle el castillo [kast**ee**-yo]

cat un gato
catch: where do we catch the bus? ¿dónde *se coge* el autobús? [dondeh seh ko-нeh el owto-booss]
  he's caught a bug ha cogido una infección [ah ko-нeedo oona eem-fekth-yon]
cathedral la catedral [kateh-dral]
catholic católico
cave una cueva [kweh-ba]
CD un CD [theh-deh]
CD-player un reproductor de CDs [reh-prodooktor deh theh-dehss]
ceiling el techo
cellophane el celofán [theh-lo-fan]
cent un céntimo [thenteemo]
centigrade centígrado [then-tee-grahdo]

✈ C/5 x 9 + 32 = F

| centigrade | -5 | 0 | 10 | 15 | 21 | 30 | 36.9 |
| Fahrenheit | 23 | 32 | 50 | 59 | 70 | 86 | 98.4 |

centimetre un centímetro [then-tee-metro]

✈ 1 cm = 0.39 inches

central central [thentral]
  with central heating con calefacción central [...kaleh-fakth-yon...]
centre el centro [th-]
  how do we get to the centre? ¿cómo se llega al centro? [...seh yeh-ga...]
centro ciudad city centre
cerrado closed
certain *(sure)* seguro [seh-goo-ro]
  are you certain? *(to man/woman)* ¿está usted seguro/a? [esta oosteh...]
certificate un certificado [thair-teefee-kahdo]
chain una cadena [ka-deh-na]
chair una silla [see-ya]

(armchair) una but**a**ca

chambermaid una camarera [kama-r**eh**-ra]

champagne el champán [tchamp**a**n]

change *(verb)* cambi**a**r

could you change this into euros? ¿puede cambiarme esto en euros? [pw**eh**deh kam-bee-**a**r-meh…**eh**-oo-ross]

I haven't any change no tengo nada suelto […sw**e**lto]

do you have change for 100 euros? ¿tiene cambio de cien euros? [tee-**eh**-neh k**a**mbee-o deh thee-**en eh**-ooross]

do we have to change trains? ¿tenemos que cambiar de tren? [teh-n**eh**-moss k…]

I'd like to change my flight ¿me puede cambiar el vuelo? [meh pw**eh**deh…el bw**eh**-lo]

I'll just get changed me voy a cambi**a**r

✈ Changing money: look for **cambio** sign; most banks accept a cheque with banker's card; write cheques in English; take your passport.

channel: the Channel el Can**a**l de la Mancha

Channel Tunnel el Eurotúnel [eh-oo-ro-t**oo**nel]

charge: what will you charge? ¿cuánto me va a cobr**a**r? [kw**a**nto meh…]

who's in charge? ¿quién está a cargo de esto? [kee-**en**…]

chart *(map)* una carta de navegación […deh na-beh-gath-y**o**n]

cheap barato [ba-r**a**hto]

have you got something cheaper? ¿tiene alguna otra cosa más barata? [tee-**eh**-neh alg**oo**na…]

cheat: I've been cheated me han engañado [meh an engan-y**ah**do]

check: will you check? ¿puede comprob**a**rlo?

[pwehdeh...]
I've checked lo he comprobado [lo eh komprobahdo]
we checked in nos inscribimos [...eenskreebeemoss]
we checked out dejamos el hotel [deh-нa-moss...]

check-in desk el mostrador de facturación [...deh faktoorath-yon]

check-in time la hora de facturación [ora deh faktoorath-yon]

cheek (of face) la mejilla [meh-нee-ya]

cheeky descarado

cheerio hasta luego [asta lweh-go]

cheers (toast) salud [saloo]
(thanks) gracias [grath-yass]

cheese el queso [keh-so]

cheeseburger una hamburguesa con queso [amboor-geh-sa kon keh-so]

chef el jefe de cocina [нeh-feh deh kotheena]

chemist's una farmacia [far-math-ya]

> ✈ A list of duty chemists (**farmacia de guar-dia**) can be found on the chemist's door or in local press. All **farmacias** are dispensing chemists, **parafarmacias** are not.

cheque un cheque [cheh-keh]
will you take a cheque? ¿aceptan cheques? [athep-tan...]

> ✈ Not standard practice and better to pay with your credit card, although you are always required to present your passport; *go to* **bank**.

cheque book el talonario de cheques [talon-ar-yo deh cheh-kess]

cheque card la tarjeta de banco [tar-нeh-ta...]

chest el pecho
chewing gum el chicle [cheek-leh]
chicken el pollo [po-yo]
chickenpox la varicela [baree-theh-la]
child un niño [neen-yo]
   (girl) una niña
child minder una niñera [neen-yeh-ra]
children los niños [neen-yoss]
   a children's portion media porción para el
   niño [mehd-ya porth-yon…]

> ✈ Children are welcome almost everywhere as
> family life is very strong in Spain.

chin la barbilla [bar-bee-ya]
china la porcelana [por-theh-lah-na]
chips unas patatas fritas [patahtass freetass]
   (in casino) las fichas [feetchass]
chocolate el chocolate [choko-lah-teh]
   a hot chocolate un chocolate a la taza […tah-
   tha]
   a box of chocolates una caja de bombones
   [kah-ʜa deh bombo-ness…]
chop: pork/lamb chop una *chuleta* de cerdo/de
   cordero [choo-lehta deh thairdo…]
Christian name el nombre de pila [nombreh deh
   peela]
Christmas Navidad [nabeeda]
   on Christmas Eve en Nochebuena [en notcheh-
   bwehna]
   Happy Christmas Feliz Navidad [feleeth…]

> ✈ Spaniards celebrate Christmas Eve as well as
> Christmas Day. Presents are given on 6th of
> January.

church una iglesia [ee-gleh-see-a]
cider un sidra [seedra]
cigar un puro [pooro]

cigarette un cigarillo [theegar**ee**-yo]

> ✈ If you prefer mild tobacco ask for **tabaco rubio** [r**oo**b-yo].

cinema el cine [th**ee**neh]

> ✈ Cheaper to go on a Wednesday although expect queues; most films are dubbed in Spanish, look for **VOS** if you want to see the film in its original language subtitled in Spanish.

circle un círculo [th**ee**rkoolo]
  (in cinema) la butaca de principal [boot**a**ka deh preen-th**ee**pa**l**]
city una ciudad [thee-oo-d**a**]
city centre el centro [th**e**n-]
claim *(insurance)* una reclamación [reklam-ath-y**o**n]
clarify aclar**a**r
clean *(adjective)* limpio [l**ee**mp-yo]
  it's not clean no está limpio
  my room hasn't been cleaned today hoy no han limpiado mi habitación [**o**y no an leemp-y**ah**do mee abee-tath-y**o**n]
cleansing cream la crema limpiad**o**ra
clear: I'm not clear about it no lo comprendo bien […bee-**e**n]
clever listo [l**ee**sto]
  (skilful) habilid**o**so
climate el clima [kl**ee**ma]
cloakroom *(for clothes)* el guardarropa [gwarda-r**o**-pa]
clock el reloj [reh-l**o**H]
close¹ cerca [th**ai**rka]
  (weather) bochorn**o**so
  is it close to…? ¿está cerca de…?
close²: when do you close? ¿a qué hora se

cierra? [ah keh **o**ra seh thee-**e**rra]

closed cerrado [ther**ah**do]

cloth la tela [t**e**h-la]

(rag) un trapo

clothes la ropa

clothes peg una pinza de la ropa [p**ee**ntha...]

cloud una nube [n**oo**beh]

clubbing: we're going clubbing vamos a ir de discotecas [b**a**moss ah eer deh deesko-t**e**hkass]

clutch el embrague [embr**a**-geh]

the clutch is slipping pat**i**na el embrague

coach un autocar [**ow**-]

coach party un grupo en autocar [...**ow**-]

coach trip una excursión (en autocar) [ess-koors-y**o**n en **ow**-]

coast la costa

at the coast en la costa

coastguard un guardacostas [gwarda-k**o**stass]

coat un abrigo [abr**ee**go]

coche-restaurante dining car

cockroach una cucaracha [kookar**a**tcha]

coffee un café [kaf**e**h]

a white coffee un café con leche [...kon l**e**h-cheh]

a black coffee un café solo

✈ Most bars serve coffee in a glass; ask for **una taza** [t**a**tha] if you want a cup. Types of coffee are:

café solo – *black*

cortado – *with a drop of milk*

café con leche – *white*

manchado – *mostly milk with drop of coffee*

Descafeinado usually implies a Nescafé® decaff sachet in hot milk (ask for **desca-feinado de máquina** if you want a proper decaff).

coin una moneda [mon**eh**-da]

coke® una Coca-Cola

cold frío [fr**ee**-o]

  I'm cold tengo frío

  I've got a cold tengo un resfriado […ress-free-**ah**do]

collapse: he's collapsed ha sufrido un colapso [ah soofr**ee**do…]

collar el cuello [kw**eh**-yo]

✈ collar sizes						
UK:	14	14.5	15	15.5	16	16.5	17
Spain:	36	37	38	39	41	42	43

collect: I've come to collect… quería recoger… [keh-r**ee**-a reh-ко**air**]

colour el color

  have you any other colours? ¿lo tiene en otros colores? [lo tee-**eh**-neh en **o**tross kol**o**ress]

comb un peine [p**ay**-neh]

come venir [ben**eer**]

  come with me venga conmigo […kon-m**ee**go]

  come here ven aquí [ben ak**ee**]

  I come from London soy de Londres

  come on! ¡vamos! [b**ah**-moss]

  oh, come on! *(disbelief)* ¡anda ya!

comedor dining room

comfortable cómodo

company *(business)* la compañía [kompan-y**ee**-a]

  you're good company lo paso genial contigo […н**e**ny**a**l kont**ee**go]

compartment *(in train)* un compartim**e**nto

compass una brújula [br**oo**-ноo-la]

compensation una indemnización [-thath-yon]

  I want compensation exijo una indemnización [egs-**ee**но…]

complain quejarse [keh-н**a**rseh]

  I want to complain about my room quiero

presentar una queja sobre mi habitación [kee-
eh-ro presentar oona keh-нa so-breh mee abee-
tath-yon]

completely completamente [komplet-amenteh]

completo full

complicated: it's very complicated es muy
complicado [...mwee komplee-kahdo]

**compliment: my compliments to the
chef** felicite al jefe de cocina de mi parte
[feleetheeteh al нeh-feh deh kotheena deh mee
parteh]

compulsory: is it compulsory? ¿es obligatorio?

computer un ordenador

concert un concierto [kon-thee-airto]

concussion una conmoción cerebral [konmoth-
yon thereh-bral]

condition *(term, state)* la condición [kondeeth-
yon]
  it's not in very good condition no está en
  muy buenas condiciones [...mwee bweh-nass
  kondeeth-yoness]

conference un congreso

confirm confirmar [konfeermar]

confuse: you're confusing me me dejas hecho
un lío [meh deh-нass etcho oon lee-o]

congratulations! ¡enhorabuena!
  [enora-bweh-na]

conjunctivitis la conjuntivitis
  [konнoonteebeeteess]

conman un estafador

connection *(travel)* el enlace [en-lah-theh]

connoisseur un experto [-pair-]
  (woman) una experta

conscious consciente [kons-thee-enteh]

consciousness: he's lost consciousness ha
perdido el conocimiento [ah pairdeedo el
konotheem-yento]

conserje porter
consigna left luggage
constipation el estreñimiento [estren-yeem-yento]
consul el/la cónsul
consulate el consulado [konsoolahdo]
contact: how can I contact...? ¿cómo puedo ponerme en contacto con...? [...pwehdo pon-airmeh...]
contact lenses las lentes de contacto [lentess...]
convenient conveniente [komben-yenteh]
cook: it's not cooked no está cocido [...kotheedo]
   you're a good cook eres un buen cocinero [airess oon bwen kotheeneh-ro]
   (to woman) eres una buena cocinera
cooker una cocina [kotheena]
cool fresco
   (great) estupendo [estoopendo]
corkscrew un sacacorchos
corner: on the corner en la esquina [...eskeena]
   in the corner en el rincón
   can we have a corner table? ¿puede darnos una mesa cerca de un rincón? [pwehdeh...mehsa thairka...]
cornflakes los copos de maíz [...mah-eeth]
correct correcto
corrida bullfight
cosmetics los cosméticos
cost: what does it cost? ¿cuánto cuesta? [kwanto kwesta]

---

   that's too much es demasiado caro [...demass-yah-do karo]
   I'll take it me lo llevo [meh lo yeh-bo]

---

cot una cuna [koona]
cotton el algodón
cotton wool el algodón

couchette una litera [leet**eh**-ra]
cough la tos [toss]
cough sweets unas pastillas para la tos
[past**ee**yass…]
could: could you…? ¿podría…? [podr**ee**-a]
could I have…? quiero… [kee-**eh**-ro]
we couldn't… no hemos podido… [no **eh**-moss
pod**ee**do]
country el país [pa-**ee**ss]
in the country(side) en el campo
couple: a couple of… *(two)* un par de…
(a few) unos pocos…/unas pocas…
courier el guía turístico [g**ee**-a…]
(woman) la guía turística
course: of course por supuesto […soopw**e**sto]
court: I'll take you to court voy a demandarle
[boy ah deh-mand**a**r-leh]
cousin: my cousin mi primo/a […pr**ee**mo/a]
cover: keep him covered manténgale *abrigado*
[mant**e**nga-leh abree-g**ah**do]
cover charge el cubierto [koob-y**air**to]
cow una vaca
crab un cangrejo [kangr**eh**-Ho]
craftshop una tienda de artesanía [tee-**e**nda deh
artesan**ee**-a]
crap: this is crap esto es una mierda […mee-
airda]
crash: there's been a crash ha habido un
accidente [ah ab**ee**do oon aktheed**e**nteh]
crash helmet un casco
crazy loco
you're crazy estás loco/a
that's crazy eso es una locura […lok**oo**ra]
cream *(on milk)* la crema [kr**eh**-ma]
(fresh) la nata
credit card una tarjeta de crédito [tar-H**eh**-ta…]
crisps: a bag of crisps una bolsa de patatas fritas

[…pat**ah**tass fr**ee**tass]
cross *(verb)* cruzar [krooth**ar**]
crossroads el cruce [kr**oo**-theh]

> ✈ Vehicles coming from the right have
> priority.

crowded abarrotado [abarot**ah**do]
cruce crossroads
cruise un crucero [kr**oo**theh-ro]
crutch *(for invalid)* una muleta [moo-l**eh**ta]
cry: don't cry no llores [no yo-ress]
cup una taza [t**a**-tha]
  a cup of coffee un café [kaf**eh**]
cupboard un armario [arm**ar**-yo]
curry el 'curry' [k**oo**-ree]
curtains las cortinas [cort**i**nas]
cushion un cojín [ko-н**ee**n]
Customs la aduana [ad-w**ah**-na]
cut cortar
  I've cut myself me he cortado [meh eh
  kort**ah**do]
cycle: can we cycle there? ¿se puede *ir en
  bicicleta*? [seh pw**eh**deh eer en beetheekl**eh**-ta]
cyclist un/una ciclista [theekl**ee**sta]
cylinder-head gasket la junta de culata [н**oo**nta
  deh kool**ah**-ta]

D [deh]

dad: my dad mi padre [p**ah**-dreh]
damage: I'll pay for the damage pagaré los
  desperfectos [-r**eh**…]
damaged defectuoso [deh-fektoo-**o**so]
damas ladies
damn! ¡maldita sea! [mal-d**ee**-ta s**eh**-a]
damp húmedo [**oo**mehdo]
dance: would you like to dance? ¿bailas

conmigo? [by-lass konm**ee**go]
dangerous pelig**ro**so
dark oscuro [-k**oo**-]
  when does it get dark? ¿a qué hora oscurece?
  [ah keh **o**ra oskoor**eh**-theh]
  dark blue azul oscuro [ath**oo**l…]
darling *(to man)* querido [keh-r**ee**do]
  (to woman) querida [keh-r**ee**da]
date: what's the date? ¿qué fecha es hoy? [keh
f**eh**-cha ess oy]
  can we make a date? *(romantic)* ¿podemos
  citarnos? [pod**eh**-moss theet**ar**-noss]

> To say the date in Spanish you just use the
> ordinary numbers (see pages 159-160). For
> 'the first' you can also say 'el primero'.

> **the first of May** el primero mayo […
> preem**air**o…]
> **in 1982** en mil novecientos ochenta y dos
> […meel nobeh-thee-**e**ntoss otchent-ɪ-d**o**ss]
> **in 2004** en dos mil cuatro […kw**a**tro]

dates *(fruit)* los dátiles [d**a**h-teeless]
daughter: my daughter mi hija [mee **ee**-нa]
day el día [d**ee**-a]
  the day after el día siguiente […seeg-y**e**nteh]
  the day before el día anterior […anteh-ree-**o**r]
dazzle: his lights were dazzling me me
  *deslumbr**a**ban* sus faros
dead muerto [mw**air**to]
deaf sordo
deal: it's a deal trato hecho […**e**tcho]
  will you deal with it? ¿puede ocuparse de
  ello? [pw**eh**deh okoop**a**r-seh deh **eh**-yo]
dear *(expensive)* caro
  Dear Francisco querido Francisco
  Dear Maria querida Maria

Dear Mr Sanchez Estimado Sr. Sanchez

December diciembre [deeth-y**e**mbreh]

deck la cubierta [koob-y**air**ta]

deckchair una tumbona [toom-b**o**-na]

declare: I have nothing to declare no tengo nada que declarar [...n**ah**-da keh deh-klar**a**r]

deep profundo

delay: the flight was delayed el vuelo *se retrasó* [bw**e**h-lo seh reh-tra-s**o**]

deliberately a propósito

delicate delicado [deleek**ah**do]

delicious delicioso [deleeth-y**o**so]

de luxe de lujo [deh l**oo**-нo]

dent una abolladura [aboya-d**oo**ra]

dentist un/una dentista

---

dentures la dentadura postiza [denta-d**oo**ra post**ee**tha]

deny: I deny it lo niego [nee-**e**h-go]

deodorant un desodorante [desodor**a**n-teh]

departure la salida [sal-**ee**da]

departure lounge la sala de embarque [... emb**a**rkeh]

depend: it depends depende [deh-p**e**ndeh]
  it depends on... depende de...

deposit *(downpayment)* una señal [sen-y**a**l]
  (security) un depósito [deh-]
  do I have to leave a deposit? ¿hay que dejar un depósito? [ɪ keh deнar...]

depressed deprim**i**do

depth la profundid**a**d [-foon-]

despacho de billetes ticket office

desperate: I'm desperate for a drink me muero

por una copa [meh mw**eh**-ro...]
dessert el postre [p**o**streh]
destination el destino
desvío diversion
detergent un detergente [detair-H**e**nteh]
detour un rodeo [rod**eh**-o]
develop: could you develop these? ¿podría
revel**ár**melas? [podr**ee**-a reh-bel**ar**-meh-lass]
diabetic diabético
diamond un diamante [dee-ah-m**a**nteh]
diarrhoea la diarrea [dee-ar**eh**-a]
  have you got something for diarrhoea?
  ¿tiene algo para la diarrea? [tee-**eh**-neh...]

> ✈ Usually caused by cold drinks or change of
> diet; drink tea or fresh lemon juice; eat only
> boiled rice, ham, apples, no fats.

diary una agenda [ah-H**e**nda]
dictionary un diccionario [deekth-yon**ar**-yo]
didn't *go to* **not**
die morir [mor**ee**r]
diesel el gas-oil
diet una dieta [dee-**eh**-ta]
  I'm on a diet estoy a dieta
different: they are different son difer**e**ntes
  can I have a different room? quisiera cambiar
  de habitación [keess-y**eh**ra kambee-**a**r deh
  abeetath-y**o**n]
difficult difícil [deef**ee**theel]
dinghy una barquita [-k**ee**-]
  (rubber) una lancha neumática [...neh-oo-
  m**a**teeka]
  (sailing) un barquito [bark**ee**to]
dining room el comedor [kom-eh-d**o**r]
dinner *(evening)* la cena [th**eh**-na]

> ✈ Normally available 9-12pm.

dinner jacket un smoking
dirección única one-way (street)
direct *(adjective)* directo [dee-]
  does it go direct? ¿va directo?
dirty sucio [sooth-yo]
disabled minusválido [mee-nooss-]
disappear desaparecer [dess-aparethair]
  it's just disappeared ha desaparecido [ah dess-aparethee-do]
disappointing decepcionante [dethepth-yonanteh]
disco una discoteca [deesko-tehka]
discount una rebaja [rebah-нa]
disgusting asqueroso [ass-keh-roso]
dish *(food, plate)* un plato
dishonest poco honrado [...on-rahdo]
disinfectant un desinfectante [-teh]
disposable camera una cámara de usar y tirar [...deh oosar ee teerar]
distance la distancia [-thee-a]
  in the distance a lo lejos [...leh-ноss]
distress signal una llamada de socorro [yamah-da...]
disturb: the noise is disturbing us nos está *molestando* el ruido [...roo-eedo]
diving board el trampolín
divorced divorciado [deeborth-yahdo]
do hacer [athair]
  what are you doing tonight? ¿qué vas a hacer esta noche? [keh bass...]
  how do you do it? ¿cómo se hace? [...seh atheh]
  will you do it for me? ¿me lo quiere hacer usted? [...kee-eh-reh athair oosteh]
  I've never done it before no lo he hecho en mi vida [...eh etcho...]
  he did it *(it was him)* lo ha hecho él [lo ah...]

I was doing 60 (kph) iba a sesenta kilómetros por hora [**ee**ba ah...**o**ra]

how do you do? hola, ¿qué tal? [**o**-la keh...]

doctor el médico

(woman) la médica

I need a doctor necesito un médico [nethess**ee**to...]

✈ A reciprocal health agreement applies with the **Seguridad Social** but NOT with private doctors; get form E111 from a post office before you go; you will have to let the Spanish doctors keep a photocopy and you will need to show your passport.

YOU MAY HEAR

¿ha tenido esto antes? *have you had this before?*

¿dónde le duele? *where does it hurt?*

¿está tomando algún medicamento? *are you taking any medication?*

tómese una/dos de éstas *take one/two of these*

cada tres horas *every three hours*

al día *every day*

dos veces al día *twice a day*

---

document un docum**e**nto [-koo-]

dog un perro

don't! ¡no lo haga! [...**ah**-ga]; *go to* **not**

door una puerta [pw**air**-ta]

dosage una dosis [d**o**seess]

double room una habitación doble [abee-tath-y**o**n d**o**bleh]

(with twin beds) una habitación con dos camas

double whisky un whisky doble [...d**o**bleh]

down: get down! ¡baje! [b**ah**-нeh]

down there ahí abajo [ah-**ee** aba-нo]

it's just down the road está un poco más abajo

downstairs abajo [ab**ah**-Ho]

drain un sumidero [soo-mee-d**eh**-ro]

drawing pin una chincheta

dress un vestido [-t**ee**do]

✈ UK:	8	10	12	14	16	18	20
Spain:	36	38	40	42	44	46	48

dressing *(for cut)* el vendaje [bend**ah**-Heh]
(for salad) el aliño [al**ee**n-yo]

drink *(verb)* beber [beb**air**]
(alcoholic) una copa
something to drink algo de beber
would you like a drink? ¿quieres beber algo? [kee-**eh**-ress…]
I don't drink no bebo [no b**eh**-bo]

drinkable: is the water drinkable? ¿es *potable* el agua? [ess pot**ah**-bleh el **ah**g-wa]

drive conducir [kondoo-th**eer**]
I've been driving all day llevo todo el día conduciendo [y**eh**-bo t**o**do el d**ee**-a kondooth-y**e**ndo]

✈ Driving in Spain: you will need registration documents, driving licence and insurance papers; seat belts compulsory; red triangle and spare set of bulbs are legal requirements.

driver el conduct**or** [-dook-]
(woman) la conduct**o**ra

driving licence el permiso de conducir [pair-m**ee**-so deh kondoo-th**eer**]

drown: he's drowning se está ahogando [seh est**a** ah-o-g**a**ndo]

drug un medicam**e**nto
(narcotic etc) una droga

drunk *(adjective)* borracho [bor**a**tcho]
dry *(adjective)* seco [s**eh**-ko]
dry-clean limpiar en seco [leemp-y**ar** en
  s**eh**-ko]
dry-cleaner's una tintorería
ducha shower
due: when is the bus due? ¿a qué hora *debe*
  llegar el autobús? [ah keh **o**ra d**eh**-beh yeh-g**ar** el
  owto-b**oo**ss]
during durante [doo-r**a**nteh]
dust el polvo
duty-free shop el 'duty-free'
DVD un DVD [deh-ooveh-d**eh**]

E [eh]

each: can we have one each? ¿nos da uno a
  cada uno? [...k**ah**da...]
  how much are they each? ¿cuánto es cada
  uno? [kw-]
ear la oreja [or**eh**-нa]
  I've got earache tengo dolor de oídos [...deh
  o-**ee**doss]
early temprano [tempr**a**hno]
  we want to leave a day earlier queremos
  irnos un día antes de lo previsto [keh-r**eh**-
  moss **ee**r-noss oon d**ee**-a **a**ntess deh lo preh-
  v**ee**sto]
earring un pendiente [pend-y**e**nteh]
east el este [**e**steh]
Easter Semana Santa [sem**ah**na...]
Easter Monday el lunes de Pascua [l**oo**ness deh
  p**a**skwa]
easy fácil [f**ah**-theel]
eat comer [kom**air**]
  something to eat algo de comer
egg un huevo [w**eh**-bo]

either: either...or... o...o...
  I don't like either no me gusta ninguno
  [...neeng**oo**no]
elastic elástico
elastic band una gomita [gom**ee**ta]
elbow el codo
electric eléctrico
electric fire una estufa eléctrica [est**oo**-fa...]
electrician un electricista [elektree-th**ee**sta]
electricity la electricidad [elektreetheed**a**]

✈ Voltage in Spain is 220 as in the UK. But
you will need a plug adaptor. Spanish plugs
have two round pins or sometimes two flat
pins.

elegant eleg**a**nte [-teh]
else: something else algo más
  somewhere else en otra parte [...-teh]
  who else? ¿quién más? [kee-**e**n...]
  or else si no
email un 'email'
  why don't you email me? ¿por qué no me
  escribes un email? [por keh no meh eskr**ee**bess...]
email address la dirección de email [deerekth-
  y**o**n...]
  what's your email address? ¿cuál es tu
  dirección de email? [kwal...]

YOU MAY THEN HEAR
  my email address is
    ...at...dot...
  mi dirección de email es
    ... arroba ... punto ...

embarrassed avergonzado [ah-bair-gon-th**ah**do]
embarrassing violento [bee-ol**e**nto]
embassy la embajada [emba**н**ada]
emergency una emergencia [em-air-**н**en-thee-a]

> ✈ dial 112 for any kind of emergency. Other emergency numbers will be given in all phone boxes.
> **policía** = police
> **bomberos** = fire brigade
> **urgencias** = medical emergencies
> **assistencia en carreteras** = motorway breakdown assistance

empty vacío [ba-th**ee**-o]

empujar push

encender luces de cruce switch headlights on

end el final [feen**a**l]
  when does it end? ¿cuándo termina? [kw**a**ndo tairrm**ee**na]

engaged *(telephone)* comunic**a**ndo [-moonee-]
  (toilet) ocupado [okoop**ah**do]
  (person) prometido [-t**ee**-]

engagement ring el anillo de prometida [an**ee**-yo...]

engine el mot**o**r

engine trouble: I've got engine trouble le pasa algo al mot**o**r [leh...]

England Inglat**e**rra

English inglés [**ee**ngl**e**ss]
  the English los ingleses [**ee**ngl**eh**-sess]

Englishman un inglés [**ee**ngl**e**ss]

Englishwoman una inglesa [**ee**ngl**eh**sa]

enjoy: I enjoyed it very much me gustó mucho [meh goost**o** m**oo**tcho]

enlargement *(photo)* una ampliación [amplee-ath-y**o**n]

enormous enorme [eh-n**o**r-meh]

enough bastante [bast**a**nteh]
  that's not big enough no es lo bastante grande
  I don't have enough money no tengo dinero bastante

thank you, that's enough gracias, vale ya
[...b**ah**-leh...]
ensuite: is it ensuite? ¿tiene baño? [tee-**eh**-neh
b**a**nyo]

✈ Spanish rooms are always ensuite, except
for cheaper hostels...

entertainment diversiones [deebairs-y**o**-ness]
entrada libre admission free
entrance la entrada [entr**ah**da]
envelope un sobre [s**o**-breh]
error un err**o**r
escalator una escalera mecánica [ess-kal**eh**-ra
meh-k**a**nika]
escuela school
especially especialmente [espeth-yal-m**e**nteh]
espere wait
essential imprescindible [eempress-theen-d**ee**bleh]
estacionamiento limitado restricted parking
e-ticket un billete electrónico [beey**eh**-teh...]
euro un euro [**eh**-ooro]
Europe Europa [eh-oor**o**-pa]
even: even the British hasta los británicos
[**a**sta...]
evening la tarde [t**a**rdeh]
(*after nightfall*) la noche [n**o**tcheh]
in the evening por la tarde/noche
this evening esta tarde/noche
good evening buenas tardes/noches [bw**eh**-
nass t**a**rdess/n**o**tchess]
evening dress (*for man*) el traje de etiqueta [tr**ah**-
Heh deh etee-k**eh**-ta]
(*for woman*) el traje de noche [...n**o**tcheh]
ever: have you ever been to...? ¿ha estado
alguna vez en...? [ah est**ah**do al-g**oo**na beth...]
every cada [k**ah**da]
every day todos los días [t**o**doss loss d**ee**-ass]

everyone todos [t**o**doss]
everything todo [t**o**do]
everywhere en todas partes [...t**o**dass p**a**rtess]
exact ex**a**cto
example un ejemplo [e**H**emplo]
  for example por ejemplo
excellent excelente [ess-thel**e**nteh]
except: except me menos yo [m**e**h-noss...]
excess baggage el exceso de equipaje [ess-th**e**h-
  so deh ekeep**a**h-**H**eh]
exchange rate el cambio [k**a**m-bee-o]
excursion una excursión [ess-koors-y**o**n]
excuse me *(to get past etc)* con permiso [...pair-
  m**ee**-so]
  (to get attention) ¡por fav**o**r!
  (apology) perdone [pair-d**o**h-neh]

> To get someone's attention you can also
> say **señor** [sen-y**o**r] to a man, **señora** [sen-
> y**o**ra] to a woman or **señorita** [sen-yor**ee**ta]
> to a younger woman.

exhaust *(on car)* el tubo de escape [t**oo**-bo deh
  esk**a**h-peh]
exhausted agotado [agot**a**hdo]
exhibition una exposición [-seeth-y**o**n]
exit la salida [-l**ee**-]
expect: she's expecting está esper**a**ndo un niño
  [...n**ee**n-yo]
expenses: it's on expenses esto corre a cargo de
  la compañía [...k**o**reh...kompan-y**ee**-a]
expensive caro [k**a**hro]
expert un experto [esp**a**irto]
  (woman) una experta
explain explic**a**r
  would you explain that slowly? ¿podría
  explicar eso lentamente? [podr**ee**-a espleek**a**r **e**h-
  so lenta-m**e**nteh]

extension cable una alargadera [-d**e**H-ra]
extra: an extra day otro día más
  is that extra? ¿eso es extra?
extremely extremadamente [estreh-mah-
  dam**e**nteh]
eye un ojo [o**H**o]
eyebrow la ceja [th**e**H-Ha]
eyebrow pencil un lápiz de cejas [l**a**peeth deh
  th**e**H-Hass]
eyeliner un lápiz de ojos [l**a**peeth deh o**H**oss]
eye shadow la sombra de ojos [...o**H**oss]
eye witness un/una testigo presencial [test**ee**go
  presenth-y**a**l]

F [**e**f-feh]

F cold
face la cara
face mask *(for diving)* unas gafas de bucear [...deh
  bootheh-**a**r]
fact el hecho [**e**tcho]
factory una fábrica
Fahrenheit 'Fahrenheit'

> ✈ F - 32 x 5/9 = C
>
> | Fahrenheit | 23 | 32 | 50 | 59 | 70 | 86 | 98.4 |
> |---|---|---|---|---|---|---|---|
> | centigrade | -5 | 0 | 10 | 15 | 21 | 30 | 36.9 |

faint: she's fainted se ha desmayado [seh ah
  dess-ma-y**a**hdo]
fair *(fun-)* una verbena [bair-b**e**h-na]
  (commercial) una feria [f**e**h-ree-a]
  that's not fair no hay derecho [no I der**e**h-cho]
fake una falsificación [-ath-y**o**n]
fall: he's fallen se ha caído [seh ah kah-**ee**do]
false falso [f**a**l-so]
false teeth los dientes postizos [dee-**e**ntess
  post**ee**-thoss]

family la familia [fam**ee**l-ya]
fan *(cooling)* un ventilador [benteela-d**o**r]
  (hand-held) un abanico [-n**ee**-]
  (supporter) un/una fan
fan belt la correa del ventilador [kor**eh**-a del
  benteela-d**o**r]
far lejos [l**eh**-Hoss]
  is it far? ¿está lejos?
  how far is it? ¿a qué distancia está? [ah keh
  deest**a**nthee-a...]
fare *(travel)* el billete [beey**eh**-teh]
farm una granja [gr**a**n-Ha]
farther más allá [...ah-y**a**]
fashion la moda
fast *(adjective)* rápido
  don't speak so fast no hable tan de prisa [no
  ah-bleh tan deh pr**ee**-sa]
fat *(adjective)* gordo
father: my father mi padre [m**ee** p**a**h-dreh]
fathom una braza [br**a**tha]
fault un defecto [deh-f**e**kto]
  it's not my fault no es culpa mía [...k**oo**lpa
  m**ee**-a]
faulty defectuoso [deh-fekt-w**o**-so]
favourite favorito [fabor**ee**to]
fax un fax
  can you fax this for me? ¿me puede mand**a**r
  esto por fax? [meh pw**eh**deh...]
February febrero [feh-br**eh**-ro]
fed-up: I'm fed-up ¡estoy harto! [...**a**rto]
feel: I feel like... *(I want)* tengo ganas de...
  [...deh]
felt-tip un rotulador [rotoola-d**o**r]
ferry el ferry
fetch: will you come and fetch me? ¿quieres
  venir a buscarme? [kee-**eh**-ress ben**ee**r ah
  boosk**a**r-meh]

fever la fiebre [fee-**eh**-breh]
few: only a few solo unos pocos/unas pocas
  a few days unos días [...d**ee**-]
fiancé el novio [n**o**-bee-o]
fiancée la novia [n**o**-bee-a]
fiddle: it's a fiddle aquí hay trampa [ak**ee ı**...]
field un campo
fifty-fifty a medias [ah m**eh**d-yass]
figs unos higos [**ee**-goss]
figure (number) la cifra [th**ee**fra]
fill: fill her up llénelo [y**eh**-neh-lo]
  to fill in a form rellenar un impreso [reh-yeh-
  n**a**r oon eempr**eh**-so]
fillet un filete [fee-l**eh**-teh]
filling (in tooth) el empaste [emp**a**steh]
film (for camera, at cinema) una película [peh-l**ee**-
  koola]
  do you have this type of film? ¿tiene películas
  de este tipo? [tee-**eh**-neh peh-l**ee**-koolass deh
  esteh t**ee**po]
filter un filtro
final de autopista end of motorway
find encontr**a**r
  if you find it si lo encuentra [see lo enkw**e**ntra]
  I've found a... he encontrado un... [eh...]
fine (weather) bueno [bw**eh**-no]
  ok, that's fine vale, muy bien [b**a**h-leh, mw**ee**
  bee-**e**n]
  a 300 euro fine una multa de trescientos euros
  [...m**oo**lta deh...eh-**oo**ross]
finger el dedo [d**eh**do]
fingernail una uña [**oo**n-ya]
finish: I haven't finished no he terminado [no eh
  tairmeen**ah**do]
  when does it finish? ¿cuándo termina?
  [kw**a**ndo tairm**ee**na]
fire un fuego [fw**eh**-go]

(*blaze: house on fire etc*) el incendio [een-th**e**ndee-o]
(*heater*) la estufa
fire! ¡fuego!
can we light a fire here? ¿se puede encender fuego aquí? [seh pw**eh**deh enthen-d**air** fw**eh**-go ak**ee**]
it's not firing (*car*) no da chispa [...ch**ee**-]
fire brigade los bomberos [bomb**eh**-ross]

✈ Dial 112 for any kind of emergency; otherwise the number for the fire brigade will be in the front of the phone directory.

fire extinguisher un extintor [esteen-t**or**]
firme deslizante slippery surface
first primero [pree-m**eh**-ro]
  I was first (*said by man/woman*) yo soy el primero/la primera
first aid primeros auxilios [pree-m**eh**-ross ah-ook-s**ee**l yoss]
first aid kit el botiquín [-k**ee**n]
first class (*travel*) primera clase [pree-m**eh**-ra kl**a**seh]
first name el nombre de pila [n**o**mbreh deh p**ee**la]
fish un pez [peth]
  (*food*) un pescado [pesk**ah**do]
fishing la pesca
fit (*healthy*) en forma
  it doesn't fit me no me vale [no meh b**a**leh]
fix: can you fix it? ¿lo puede arreglar? [... pw**eh**deh...]
fizzy con gas
flag la bandera [band**eh**-ra]
flash (*photography*) un flash
flat (*adjective*) llano [y**ah**-no]
  (*apartment*) un piso [p**ee**-so]

I've got a flat (tyre) tengo una (rueda) deshinchada [...rw*eh*-da dess-eench*ah*-da]

flavour el sabor [sa-b*or*]

flea una pulga [p*oo*lga]

flies *(on trousers)* la bragueta [-g*eh*-]

flight el vuelo [bw*eh*-lo]

flight number el número de vuelo [n*oo*-meh-ro deh bw*eh*-lo]

flippers unas aletas [al*eh*tass]

flirt *(verb)* coquetear [kokeh-teh-*ar*]

float *(verb)* flotar

floor el suelo [sw*eh*-lo]

   on the second floor en el segundo *piso* [...p*ee*-so]

flower una flor

flu la gripe [gr*ee*peh]

fly *(verb)* volar [bol*ar*]

   (insect) una mosca

foggy: it's foggy hay niebla [ɪ nee-y*eh*-bla]

follow seguir [-g*ee*r]

food la comida [kom*ee*da]

food poisoning una intoxicación alimenticia [intoxeekath-y*o*n aleement*ee*th-ya]

fool un tonto

   (woman) una tonta

foot un pie [pee-*eh*]

  ✈ 1 foot = 30.5 cm = 0.3 metres

football *(game)* el fútbol

   (ball) un balón

for para

   that's for me es para mí

forbidden prohibido [pro-eeb*ee*do]

foreign extranjero [-H*eh*-ro]

foreign currency las divisas [dee-b*ee*-sass]

foreigner un extranjero [-H*eh*-ro]

   (woman) una extranjera

forest un bosque [boskeh]
forget olvidar [olbee-dar]
  I forget no me acuerdo [no meh ak-wairdo]
  I've forgotten me he olvidado [meh eh olbeedahdo]
  don't forget no se olvide [...-bee-deh]
fork *(to eat with)* un tenedor [teneh-dor]
form *(document)* una hoja [o-нa]
formal *(person)* estirado [esteerahdo]
  (dress) de etiqueta [eteekeh-ta]
fortnight quince días [keen-theh dee-ass]
forward *(move etc)* hacia adelante [ath-ya adelanteh]
  could you forward my mail? ¿puede enviarme el correo a mi nueva dirección? [pwehdeh embee-armeh el koreh-o ah mee nweh-ba deerekth-yon]
forwarding address la nueva dirección [nweh-ba deerekth-yon]
foundation cream una crema base [kreh-ma bah-seh]
fountain una fuente [fwenteh]
four-wheel drive un todo terreno [...tereh-no]
fracture una fractura [fraktoora]
fragile frágil [frah-нeel]
France Francia [franth-ya]
fraud un fraude [fra-oo-deh]
free libre [leebreh]
  (no charge) gratis [grah-teess]
  admission free entrada gratis
freight las mercancías [-thee-ass]
French francés [fran-thess]
fresh fresco
freshen up: I'd like to freshen up quiero refrescarme [kee-eh-ro reh-freskar-meh]
Friday viernes [bee-air-ness]
fridge el frigorífico

fried egg un huevo frito [weh-bo freeto]
friend un amigo [ameego]
  (female) una amiga
friendly simpático
fries unas patatas fritas [patahtass freetass]
frio cold
from de [deh]
  where is it from? ¿de dónde es?

> **De** when used with **el** becomes **del**.
>   **from the airport** del aeropuerto

front: in front of you *delante* de usted [delanteh
  deh oosteh]
  at the front por delante
fruit la fruta [froota]
fruit salad una macedonia de frutas [mathedon-
  ya deh frootass]
fry freír [freh-eer]
  nothing fried nada frito
frying pan una sartén
full lleno [yeh-no]
fun: it's fun es divertido […deebair-teedo]
  have fun! ¡que te diviertas! [keh teh deeb-
  yairtass]
funny *(strange)* raro [rah-ro]
  (comical) gracioso [grath-yo-so]
furniture los muebles [mweh-bless]
further más allá […ah-yah]
fuse el fusible [foo-see-bleh]
future el futuro [footoo-ro]
  in the future en lo sucesivo […soo-thess-eebo]

G [Heh]

gale un vendaval
gallon un galón

✈ 1 gallon = 4.55 litres

gallstone un cálculo biliario [kalkoolo beel-yaree-yo]

gamble jugar [Hoogar]

garage *(for repairs)* un taller [ta-yair]
  (for petrol) una gasolinera [-eeneh-ra]
  (for parking) un garage [gara-Heh]

garden el jardín [Hardeen]

garlic el ajo [ah-Ho]

gas el gas
  (petrol) la gasolina [-lee-]

gas cylinder una bombona de gas

gasket una junta [Hoonta]

gay 'gay' [gI]

gear *(in car)* la marcha
  (equipment) el equipo [-kee-]
  I can't get it into gear no le entra la marcha

gents los aseos [asseh-oss]

Germany Alemania [aleh-man-ya]

gesture un gesto [Hesto]

get: will you get me a...? ¿me quiere buscar un/una...? [meh kee-eh-reh booskar...]
  how do I get to...? ¿cómo se va a...?
  where do I get a bus for...? ¿dónde se coge el autobús para...? [dondeh seh ko-Heh el owto-booss...]
  when can I get it back? ¿cuándo puedo recogerlo? [...pwehdo rehko-Hair-lo]
  when do we get back? ¿a qué hora volvemos? [ah keh ora bolbehmoss]
  where do I get off? ¿dónde tengo que bajarme? [...baHarmeh]
  have you got...? ¿tiene...? [tee-eh-neh]

gin una ginebra [Heeneh-bra]

gin and tonic una tónica con ginebra

girl una chica [cheeka]

girlfriend la amiga
give dar
  will you give me...? ¿me quiere dar...? [meh
  kee-**eh**-reh...]
  I gave it to him se lo dí a él [...dee...]
glad cont**e**nto
  I'm glad me alegro
glass el crist**a**l
  (drinking) un vaso [b**ah**-so]
  a glass of wine un vaso de vino
glasses las gafas
glue la cola
go ir [eer]

> Here is the present tense of the verb 'to go'.
>
> **I go** v**o**y [boy]
> **you go** *(familiar)* vas [bass]
> **you go** *(polite)* va [ba]
> **he/she/it goes** va
> **we go** vamos [b**a**moss]
> **you go** *(familiar plural)* vais [v**a**-eess]
> **you go** *(polite plural)* van [ban]
> **they go** van

  does this go to the airport? ¿va al aeropuerto?
  [ba...]
  when does the bus go? ¿a qué hora sale el
  autobús? [ah keh **o**ra s**ah**-leh el owto-b**oo**ss]
  the bus has gone se nos ha ido el autobús
  [...ah **ee**do...]
  he's gone se ha ido [seh...]
  where are you going? ¿dónde vas? [d**o**ndeh
  bass]
  let's go vámonos [b**ah**-monoss]
  go on! ¡venga ya! [b**e**nga...]
  can I have a go? ¿puedo prob**a**r yo?
  [pw**eh**do...]

goal un gol
goat's cheese el queso de cabra [k**eh**-so...]
God Dios [dee-**oss**]
gold el oro
golf el golf
golf course el campo de golf
good bueno [bw**eh**-no]
 good! ¡muy bien! [mw**ee** bee-**en**]
goodbye adiós
got: have you got...? ¿tiene...? [tee-**eh**-neh]
gram un gramo
granddaughter la nieta [nee-**eh**ta]
grandfather el abuelo [abw**eh**-lo]
grandmother la abuela [abw**eh**-la]
grandson el nieto [nee-**eh**to]
grapefruit un pomelo [pom**eh**-lo]
grapefruit juice un zumo de pomelo [th**oo**mo
 deh pom**eh**-lo]
grapes unas uvas [**oo**bass]
grass la hierba [y**air**-ba]
grateful: I'm very grateful to you se lo
 agradezco mucho [seh lo agrad**eth**-ko...]
gravy la salsa
grease la grasa
greasy grasiento [grass-y**en**to]
great grande [gr**an**deh]
 (very good) estupendo [estoop**en**do]
 great! ¡estupendo!
Greece Grecia [gr**eth**-ya]
greedy codicioso [kodeethee-**o**so]
 (for food) glotón
green verde [b**air**-deh]
grey gris [greess]
grocer's la tienda de comestibles [tee-**en**da deh
 komest**ee**-bless]
ground el suelo [sw**eh**-lo]
 on the ground en el suelo

on the ground floor en la planta baja [...bah-нa]
group un grupo [groopo]
  our group leader el/la guía de nuestro grupo [gee-a deh nwestro...]
  I'm with the English group estoy en el grupo de los ingleses [...eengleh-sess]
guarantee una garantía [-tee-a]
  is there a guarantee? ¿tiene garantía? [tee-eh-neh...]
guest un invitado [eembeetahdo]
  (woman) una invitada
  (in hotel) un/una huésped [wespeth]
guesthouse una casa de huéspedes [kah-sa deh wespedess]
guide un/una guía [gee-a]
guidebook una guía [gee-a]
guided tour una visita con guía [bee-seeta kon gee-a]
guilty culpable [koolpah-bleh]
guitar una guitarra [geetara]
gum *(in mouth)* la encía [enthee-a]
gun *(pistol)* una pistola
gypsy un gitano [Heetahno]
  (woman) una gitana

H [atcheh]

hair el pelo [peh-lo]
haircut un corte de pelo [korteh deh peh-lo]
hairdresser's: is there a hairdresser's here? ¿hay alguna *peluquería* aquí? [ɪ algoona pelookeh-ree-a akee]
hair grip una horquilla [or-kee-ya]
half la mitad [meeta]
  a half portion una media porción [mehd-ya porth-yon]

half an hour media hora [mehd-ya ora]
  go to **time**
ham el jamón de York [Hamon…]
hamburger una hamburguesa [amboor-geh-sa]
hammer un martillo [marteeyo]
hand una mano
handbag un bolso
hand baggage el equipaje de mano [ekee-pah-Heh…]
handbrake el freno de mano [freh-no…]
handkerchief un pañuelo [pan-yweh-lo]
handle el picaporte [peeka-porteh]
  (of cup) el asa
handmade hecho a mano [etcho…]
handsome guapo [gwah-po]
hanger una percha [pair-cha]
hangover una resaca [reh-saka]
happen suceder [sootheh-dair]
  I don't know how it happened no sé cómo
  sucedió […seh…soothehd-yo]
  what's happening? ¿qué pasa? [keh…]
  what's happened? ¿qué ha pasado? [keh ah…]
happy contento
harbour el puerto [pwairto]
hard duro [dooro]
  (difficult) difícil [deefeetheel]
hard-boiled egg un huevo duro [weh-bo dooro]
harm el daño [dan-yo]
hat un sombrero
hate: I hate… detesto… [deh-testo]
have *(possess)* tener [tenair]
  (breakfast, lunch) tomar
  can I have…? ¿me da…? [meh…]
  can I have some water? ¿puede ponerme un
  poco de agua? [pwehdeh po-nair-meh…]
  I have no… no tengo… [no teng-go]
  do you have any cigars/a map? ¿tiene puros/

un mapa? [tee-**eh**-neh…]
I have to leave tomorrow tengo que irme
mañana [**t**eng-go keh **ee**r-meh man-y**ah**-na]

> Here is the present tense of the verb for
> 'to have'.
>
> **I have** tengo [t**e**ng-go]
> **you have** tienes *(familiar)* [tee-**eh**-ness]
> **you have** tiene *(polite)* [tee-**eh**-neh]
> **he/she/it has** tiene [tee-**eh**-neh]
> **we have** tenemos [ten-**eh**moss]
> **you have** tenéis *(familiar plural)* [ten-**eh**-eess]
> **you have** tienen *(polite plural)* [tee-**eh**-nen]
> **they have** tienen [tee-**eh**-nen]

> Another very common way of expressing
> 'have to' is with **hay que** [ɪ keh].
> **¿hay que pagar?** do you/I/we have to
> pay?

hay fever la fiebre del heno [fee-**eh**-breh del **eh**-
no]
he él

> If there is no special emphasis Spanish
> doesn't use the word **él**.
> **does he live here?** ¿vive aquí? [b**ee**-beh
> ak**ee**]

head la cabeza [kab**eh**-tha]
headache un dol**o**r de cabeza […kab**eh**-tha]
headlight el faro

> ✈ Flashing headlights mean 'stop' or 'get out
> of my way' and NOT 'after you, chum' as
> in the UK.

head waiter el maître [metr]
head wind un viento contrario [bee-**e**nto kontr**ah**-

ree-yo]

health la salud [sal**oo**]

　your health! ¡a tu salud! [ah too...]

hear: I can't hear no oigo [no **oy**-go]

hearing aid un apar**a**to del oído [...o-**ee**do]

heart el corazón [korath**o**n]

heart attack un infarto

heat el calor [ka-l**o**r]

heating la calefacción [kaleh-fakth-y**o**n]

heat stroke una insolación [-lath-y**o**n]

heavy pesado [peh-s**ah**do]

heel el talón

　(of shoe) el tacón

　could you put new heels on these? ¿puede
　ponerles tapas nuevas? [pw**eh**deh pon**air**-less
　t**a**pass nw**eh**-bass]

height la altura [-t**oo**-]

hello ¡hola! [**o**-la]

　(to get attention) ¡oiga! [**oy**ga]

　(answering the phone) ¿diga?

help la ayuda [-y**oo**-]

　can you help me? ¿puede ayudarme?
　[pw**eh**deh ah-yoo-d**a**r-meh]

　help! ¡soc**o**rro!

her¹: I know her *la* conozco [...kon**o**th-ko]

　will you give it to her? ¿quiere dárselo a *ella*?
　[kee-**eh**-reh d**a**rseh-lo a **eh**-ya]

　with/for her con/para ella

　it's her es ella

　who? – her ¿quién? – ella

her² *(possessive)* su [soo]

> No feminine ending; plural is **sus**. Since **su**
> can also mean 'his', 'your' and 'their' you
> can specify with **de ella**:
> 　**but which is her car?** ¿pero cuál es el
> 　coche de ella? [kwal...deh **eh**-ya]

here aquí [ak**ee**]
  come here ven aquí [ben…]
hers suyo/suya [s**oo**-yo…]
hi! ¡hola! [**o**-la]
high alto
  higher up más arriba […ar**ee**ba]
high chair una silla alta [s**ee**-ya…]
hill un monte [m**o**nteh]
  (on road) una cuesta [kw**e**sta]
  up/down the hill cuesta arriba/abajo [kw**e**sta
  ar**ee**ba/ab**ah**-HO]
him: I know him *le* conozco [leh kon**o**th-ko]
  will you give it to him? ¿quiere dárselo a *él*?
  [kee-**eh**-reh…]
  it's him es él
  with/for him con/para él
  who? – him ¿quién? – él
hire *go to* **rent**
his su [soo]

> No feminine ending; plural is **sus**. Since **su**
> can also mean 'her', 'your' and 'their' you
> can specify with **de él**.
>   **that's not his car** ése no es el coche de él
>   **it's his** es suyo […s**oo**yo]

hit: he hit me me golpeó [meh golpeh-**o**]
hitch-hike hacer autostop [ath**ai**r owto-st**o**p]
hitch-hiker un/una autostopista [owto-stop**ee**sta]
hitch-hiking el autostop [owto-st**o**p]
hold *(verb)* tener [ten**ai**r]
hole un agujero [agoo-H**eh**-ro]
holiday las vacaciones [bakath-y**o**ness]
  (single day) un día festivo […fest**ee**bo]
  I'm on holiday estoy de vacaciones
Holland Holanda
home la casa [k**ah**-sa]
  at home en casa

(back in Britain) en nuestro país [...pa-ee*ss*]
I want to go home quiero irme a casa [kee-**eh**-ro **ee**r-meh...]
homesick: I'm homesick tengo morriña [...mor**ee**n-ya]
honest honrado [onr**ah**do]
honestly? ¿de verdad? [deh baird**a**]
honey la miel [mee-**e**l]
honeymoon el viaje de novios [bee-**ah**-Heh deh n**o**bee-oss]
hope la esperanza [-**a**ntha]
  I hope that... espero que... [esp**eh**-ro keh]
  I hope so espero que sí
  I hope not espero que no
horas de visita visiting hours
horn *(of car)* el cl**a**xon
horrible horrible [or**ee**bleh]
horse un caballo [kab**a**-yo]
hospital el hospital [ospeet**a**l]

→ Look for **Urgencias** – A&E; *go to* **doctor**.

host el anfitrión [amfeetree-**o**n]
hostess la anfitri**o**na
hot caliente [kal-y**e**nteh]
  (spiced) picante [peek**a**nteh]
  I'm so hot! ¡tengo tanto calor! [...ka-l**o**r]
  it's so hot today! ¡hoy hace tanto calor! [oy **a**theh...]
hotel un hotel [o-t**e**l]
  at my hotel en mi hotel

→ Apart from hotels there are also **hostales** and **pensiones** (boarding houses) often cheaper and quite adequate with meals available. Get a list of hotels etc from the local tourist office or **oficina de turismo** (includes price list). Look for the sign **HR** for rock-bottom prices. At the top end there is a **parador**, usually in a historical or scenic location.

hour una hora [**o**ra]
house una casa [k**ah**-sa]
how cómo
  how many? ¿cuántos?[kw-]
  how much? ¿cuánto?
  how much is it? ¿cuánto es?
  how long does it take? ¿cuánto se tarda?
  how long have you been here? ¿desde cuándo estás aquí? [d**e**zdeh kw**a**ndo est**a**ss ak**ee**]
  how are you? ¿cómo está usted? [...oost**eh**]

  YOU MAY THEN HEAR
  muy bien gracias *very well thanks*
  así así *so-so*

humid húmedo [**oo**meh-do]
hungry: I'm hungry tengo hambre [...**a**mbreh]
  I'm not hungry no tengo hambre
hurry: I'm in a hurry tengo prisa [...pr**ee**-sa]
  please hurry! ¡de prisa, por fav**o**r!
hurt: it hurts me duele [meh dw**eh**-leh]
  my leg hurts me duele la pierna [...pee-**air**-na]
husband el marido [mar**ee**do]

I [ee]

I yo

  If there is no special emphasis Spanish doesn't use the word **yo**.
    I am tired estoy cansado

ice el hielo [y**eh**-lo]
  with lots of ice con mucho hielo
ice cream un helado [eh-l**ah**do]

iced coffee un café helado [kafeh eh-lahdo]
identity papers los documentos de identidad
   [dokoomentoss deh eedentee-da]
idiot un/una idiota [eed-yota]
if si [see]
ignition *(of car)* el encendido [enthendeedo]
ill enfermo [enfairmo]
   I feel ill me encuentro mal [me enkwentro...]
illegal ilegal [ee-leh-gal]
illegible ilegible [ee-leh-Hee-bleh]
illness una enfermedad [enfairmeh-da]
immediately ahora mismo [ah-ora meezmo]
important importante [-teh]
   it's very important es muy importante [...
   mwee...]
impossible imposible [-seebleh]
impressive impressionante [eempress-yonanteh]
improve mejorar [meHorar]
   I want to improve my Spanish quiero
   perfeccionar mi español [kee-eh-ro pairfekth-
   yonar mee espan-yol]
in en
   is he in? ¿está?
inch una pulgada [poolgahda]

✈ 1 inch = 2.54 cm

include incluír [eenkloo-eer]
   does that include breakfast? ¿está incluido el
   desayuno? [...eenkloo-eedo el dessa-yoono]
incompetent incompetente [-teh]
inconsiderate desconsiderado
incredible increíble [een-kreh-eebleh]
indecent indecente [een-deh-thenteh]
independent independiente [eendeh-pend-
   yenteh]
India India
indicate: he turned without indicating giró

sin *señalar* [нee-r**o** seen sen-yal**a**r]
indicator *(on car)* el indicad**o**r

> ✈ Spanish lorry drivers sometimes indicate
> right to let you know it's safe to overtake;
> indicating left will mean it's not safe.

indigestion la indigestión [eendee-нest-y**o**n]
indoors en casa [k**ah**-sa]
infection una infección [eenfekth-y**o**n]
infectious infeccioso [eenfekth-y**o**-so]
information la información [-ath-y**o**n]
  **do you have any information in English
  about...?** ¿tiene alguna información en inglés
  sobre...? [tee-**eh**-neh algoona...s**o**-breh]
  is there an information office? ¿hay una
  oficina de información? [**i** oona ofee-th**ee**na
  deh...]
injection una inyección [een-yekth-y**o**n]
injured herido [eh-r**ee**do]
injury una herida [eh-r**ee**-da]
innocent inocente [-th**e**nteh]
insect un ins**e**cto
insect repellent una loción antimosquitos [loth-
  y**o**n...]
inside dentro de [...deh]
insist: I insist insisto [eens**ee**sto]
insomnia el insomnio [een-s**o**mnee-o]
instant coffee un café instantáneo [kaf**eh**
  eenstant**ah**-neh-o]
instead en cambio [en k**a**m-bee-o]
  instead of... en lugar de... [en loog**a**r deh]
insulating tape una cinta aislante [th**e**enta ah-
  eess-l**a**nteh]
insult un insulto [eens**oo**lto]
insurance el seguro [seh-g**oo**ro]
insurance company la compañía de seguros
  [kompan-y**ee**-a deh seg**oo**ross]

intelligent inteligente [eentelee-нenteh]
interesting interesante [eenteh-reh-santeh]
international internacional [eentair-nath-yonal]
Internet el Internet [eentairnet]
Internet café un cibercafé [theebair-kafeh]
interpret interpretar
  would you interpret for us? ¿podría hacer de intérprete nuestro? [podree-a athair deh eentair-preteh nwestro]
interpreter un/una intérprete [eentairpreh-teh]
into en
  I'm not into that a mí eso no me gusta [...eh-so no meh goosta]
  introduce: can I introduce...? permítame *presentarle* a... [pairmeeta-meh press-entar-leh ah]
invalid un inválido [eembalido]
  (woman) una inválida
invitation una invitación [eembeetath-yon]
  thanks for the invitation gracias por la invitación

✈ Better take something for dessert rather than a bottle of wine, if you're invited to someone's house for a meal.

invite: can I invite you out? ¿te gustaría salir conmigo? [teh goostaree-a saleer konmeego]
Ireland Irlanda [eerlanda]
Irish irlandés [eerlandess]
Irishman un irlandés [eerlandess]
Irishwoman una irlandesa [eerlandeh-sa]
iron *(for clothes)* una plancha
  will you iron these for me? ¿puede plancharmelos? [pwehdeh planchar-meh-loss]
is *go to* **be**
island una isla [eesla]
it lo/la

Use **lo** or **la** depending on whether the noun is **el** or **la**.
  give it to me démelo/démela [d**eh**-meh-lo…]

As the subject of a sentence Spanish has no translation for 'it'.
  is it? ¿es…?, ¿está…?
  it's not working no funciona […foonth-y**o**-na]

Italy Italia
itch: it itches me pica [meh p**ee**ka]
itemize: would you itemize it for me? ¿me lo puede desglosar? [meh lo pw**eh**deh dez-glo-s**a**r]

J [H**o**ta]

jack *(for car)* el gato
jacket una chaqueta [chak**eh**-ta]
jam la mermelada [mair-meh-l**ah**-da]
  traffic jam un atasco
January enero [en-**eh**-ro]
jaw la mandíbula [-d**ee**boo-]
jealous *(in love)* celoso [thel**o**so]
jeans los vaqueros [bak**eh**-ross]
jellyfish una medusa [med**oo**sa]
jetty el muelle [mw**eh**-yeh]
jewellery las joyas [H**o**y-yass]
job un trabajo [traba-Ho]
  just the job ¡estupendo! [es-too-p**e**ndo]
joke un chiste [ch**ee**steh]
  you must be joking! ¿pero lo dices en serio? [p**eh**-ro lo d**ee**thess en s**eh**-ree-o]
journey el viaje [bee-a**Heh**]
  have a good journey! ¡buen viaje! [bw**en**…]
July julio [H**oo**l-yo]

junction un cruce [kr**oo**-theh]
  (on motorway) un nudo [n**oo**do]
June junio [H**OO**n-yo]
junk baratijas [barat**ee**-Hass]
  (food) porquerías [porkeh-r**ee**-ass]
just *(only)* sólo
  (exactly) justo [H**OO**sto]
  just a little sólo un poquito […pok**ee**to]
  not just now no en este momento […est**eh**…]
  just now ahora mismo [ah-**o**ra m**ee**zmo]
  he was here just now est**a**ba aquí hace un
  momento […ak**ee a**theh…]
  that's just right así está bién […bee-**e**n]

K [ka]

keep: can I keep it? ¿puedo quedarme con él?
  [pw**eh**do keh-d**a**r-meh…]
  you keep it quédese con él [k**eh**-deh-seh…]
  keep the change quédese con el cambio
  you didn't keep your promise no cumplió su
  promesa [no koomplee-**o** soo prom-**eh**-sa]
key la llave [y**a**h-beh]
keycard una tarjeta llave [tarH**eh**ta y**a**beh]
kidney el riñón [reen-y**o**n]
kill mat**a**r
kilo un kilo [k**ee**lo]

✈ kilos/5 x 11 = pounds

kilos	1	1.5	5	6	7	8	9
pounds	2.2	3.3	11	13.2	15.4	17.6	19.8

kilometre un kilómetro [keel**o**metro]

✈ kilometres/8 x 5 = miles

kilometres	1	5	10	20	50	100
miles		0.62	3.11	6.2	12.4	31	62

kind: that's very kind of you es usted muy

amable [ess oost**eh** mwee am**ah**-bleh]
  what kind of...? ¿qué tipo de...? [keh t**ee**po deh]
kiss un beso [b**eh**-so]
  (verb) besar [beh-s**ar**]

> ✈ The normal form of greeting between friends and new acquaintances (woman/woman or man/woman).

kitchen la cocina [koth**ee**na]
knee una rodilla [rod**ee**-ya]
knife un cuchillo [kooch**ee**-yo]
knock *(verb: at door)* llamar [yam**ar**]
  there's a knocking noise from the engine suena un golpeteo en el motor [sw**eh**-na oon golpeh-t**eh**-o...]
know saber [sab**air**]
  (person, place) conocer [konoth**air**]
  I don't know no sé [no seh]
  I didn't know no lo sabía [...sab**ee**-a]
  I don't know the area no conozco la región [no kon**o**thko la reн-y**o**n]

L [**eh**-leh]

label la etiqueta [-eek**eh**-ta]
laces unos cordones [kord**o**-ness]
lacquer la laca [la l**a**ca]
ladies (toilet) los aseos de señoras [ass-**eh**-oss deh sen-y**o**rass]
lady una señora [sen-y**o**ra]
lager una cerveza [thair-b**eh**-tha]

> ✈ If you ask for **cerveza** you will automatically be served lager-type beer, although very cold and maybe sharper-tasting than you're used to.

a lager and lime una cerveza con lima [...leema]

✈ Very unusual. You could try shandy (ask for **una clara**).

lake el lago
lamb *(meat)* el cordero [-deh-]
lamp una lámpara
lamppost una farola
lampshade una pantalla [panta-ya]
land la tierra [tee-era]
lane *(on road)* el carril [kareel]
language el idioma [eed-yo-ma]
language course un curso de idiomas [...deh eed-yo-mass]
laptop un ordenador portátil [...portahteel]
large grande [grandeh]
laryngitis la laringitis [lareen-Heeteess]
last último [oolteemo]
  last year el año pasado [an-yo pass-ahdo]
  last week la semana pasada
  last night anoche [anotcheh]
  at last! ¡al fin! [...feen]
late tarde [tardeh]
  sorry I'm late perdone que haya llegado tarde [pair-do-neh keh ah-ya yeh-gahdo tardeh]
  it's a bit late es un poco tarde
  please hurry, I'm late dése prisa, por favor, que llego tarde [deh-seh pree-sa...keh yeh-go tardeh]
  at the latest a más tardar
later más tarde [...tardeh]
  see you later hasta luego [asta lweh-go]
laugh *(verb)* reír [reh-eer]
launderette una lavandería automática [-ree-a owto-mateeka]

✈ Only in large cities or holiday resorts.

lavabos toilets
lavatory el wáter [b**ah**-tair]
law la ley [lay]
lawyer un abogado [abog**ah**do]
 (woman) una abogada
laxative un laxante [-**a**nteh]
lazy perezoso [peh-reth**o**so]
leaf una hoja [**o**-Ha]
leak un agujero [agoo-H**e**h-ro]
 it leaks se sale [seh s**ah**leh]
learn: I want to learn... quiero aprender... [kee-**e**h-ro aprend**air**]
lease *(verb)* alquiler [alkeel**air**]
 (land) arrend**a**r
least: not in the least de ninguna manera [deh neeng**oo**na man**e**h-ra]
 at least por lo menos [...m**e**hnoss]
leather el cuero [kw**e**h-ro]
leave *(go away)* irse [**ee**rseh]
 we're leaving tomorrow nos vamos mañana
 when does the bus leave? ¿a qué hora sale el autobús? [ah keh **o**-ra s**ah**-leh el owto-b**oo**ss]
 I left two shirts in my room me dejé dos camisas en mi habitación [meh deH**eh** doss kam**ee**-sass en mee abee-tath-y**o**n]
 can I leave this here? ¿puedo dejar esto aquí? [pw**eh**do deH**a**r **e**sto ak**ee**]
left izquierdo [eeth-kee-**air**do]
 on the left a la izquierda
left-handed zurdo [th**oo**rdo]
left luggage (office) la consigna de equipajes [kons**ee**g-na deh ekeep**ah**-Hess]
leg la pierna [pee-**air**-na]
legal *(permitted)* legal [leh-g**a**l]
lemon un limón [leem**o**n]

lemonade limonada [leemon*ah*da]
lend: will you lend me your...? ¿quiere
prestarme su...? [kee-*eh*-reh prest*a*r-meh soo]
lens *(for camera)* el objetivo [ob-ʜeh-t*ee*bo]
(of glasses) la lente [l*e*nteh]
less menos [m*eh*-noss]
less than that menos que eso [...keh...]
let: let me help déjeme ayudarle [d*e*ʜeh-meh ah-
yood*a*r-leh]
let me go! ¡suélteme! [sw*e*l-teh-meh]
will you let me off here? déjeme aquí, por
favor [d*e*ʜeh-meh ak*ee*...]
let's go vámonos [b*ah*-monoss]
letter una carta
(of alphabet) la letra
are there any letters for me? ¿hay cartas para
mí? [ɪ...mee]
letterbox un buzón [boo-th*o*n]

✈ Letterboxes are yellow.

lettuce una lechuga [-ch*oo*-]
level crossing el paso a nivel [...ah neeb*e*l]
liable *(responsible)* responsable [-s*ah*-bleh]
library la biblioteca [beeb-lee-o-t*eh*-ka]
licence un permiso [pair-m*ee*-so]
lid la tapa
lie *(untruth)* una mentira [-t*ee*-]
can he lie down for a bit? ¿puede acostarse
un rato? [pw*e*hdeh akost*a*r-seh...]
life la vida [b*ee*da]
that's life así es la vida [as*ee*...]
lifebelt el salvavidas [-b*ee*dass]
lifeboat la lancha salvavidas [...-b*ee*dass]
lifeguard un/una socorrista [-*ee*sta]
life insurance un seguro de vida [seh-g*oo*ro...]
life jacket el salvavidas [-b*ee*dass]
lift: do you want a lift? ¿quiere que le lleve en

mi coche? [kee-**eh**-reh keh leh y**eh**-beh en mee k**o**tcheh]
could you give me a lift? ¿podría llevarme en su coche? [pod-r**ee**-a yeh-b**a**r-meh…]
the lift isn't working no funciona el *ascensor* [no foonth-y**o**na el ass-thens**o**r]
light *(not heavy)* ligero [lee-н**e**h-ro]
  the light la luz [looth]
  have you got a light? ¿tiene fuego? [tee-**e**h-neh fw**e**h-go]
  the lights aren't working no funcionan las luces [no foonth-y**o**nan lass l**oo**thess]
  light blue azul claro [ath**oo**l kl**a**h-ro]
light bulb una bombilla [-b**ee**ya]
lighter un encendedor [enthendeh-d**o**r]
like: would you like…? ¿quiere…? [kee-**e**h-reh]
  I'd like a… quisiera un/una… [keess-y**e**h-ra…]
  I'd like to… quisiera…
  I like it me gusta [meh g**oo**sta]
  I like you me gustas
  I don't like it no me gusta
  what's it like? ¿cómo es?
  do it like this hágalo así [**a**h-galo as**ee**]
  one like that uno como ése […**e**h-seh]
lime una lima [l**ee**ma]
lime juice un zumo de lima [th**oo**mo deh l**ee**ma]
line una línea [l**ee**-neh-a]
lip el labio [l**a**hb-yo]
lip salve una crema labial [kr**e**hma lahb-y**a**l]
lipstick una barra de labios […l**a**hb-yoss]
liqueur un lic**o**r

✈ You could try:
  aguardiente [agwardee-**e**nteh] clear fruit-based brandy; not only literally 'firewater'.
  pacharán a wild cherry liqueur
  anís anisette

list una lista [**lee**sta]
listen escuchar [eskoo**char**]
  listen! ¡oye! [**o**-yeh]
litre un litro [**lee**tro]

✈ 1 litre = 1.75 pints = 0.22 gals

little pequeño [pek**eh**n-yo]
  a little ice un poco de hielo [...**yeh**-lo]
  a little more un poco más
  just a little sólo un poquito [...pok**ee**to]
live vivir [beeb**eer**]
  I live in Glasgow vivo en Glasgow
  where do you live? ¿dónde vives? [d**o**ndeh
  b**ee**bess]
liver el hígado [**ee**gahdo]
lizard un lagarto
llegadas arrivals
loaf una barra
lobster una langosta
local: could we try a local wine? quisiéramos
  probar un vino *de esta zona* [keess-y**eh**-ramoss
  pro-b**ar** oon...th**o**-na]
  a local restaurant un restaurante del barrio
  [rest-ow-r**a**nteh del b**a**ree-o]
lock: the lock's broken está rota la *cerradura*
  [...therad**oo**ra]
  I've locked myself out no puedo entrar porque
  me he dejado la llave dentro [no pw**eh**do
  entr**ar** p**o**rkeh meh eh deh-н**ah**do la y**ah**-beh
  d**e**ntro]
London Londres [l**o**ndress]
lonely solitario [-t**a**r-yo]
long largo
  a long time mucho tiempo [m**oo**tcho tee-**e**mpo]
  we'd like to stay longer nos gustaría
  quedarnos más tiempo [noss goostar**ee**-a keh-
  d**a**rnoss mass tee-**e**mpo]

loo: where's the loo? ¿dónde está el wáter?
[...b**ah**-tair]
look: you look tired pareces cansado/a [par**eh**-
thess...]
  look at that mire eso [m**ee**-reh **eh**-so]
  can I have a look? ¿puedo ver? [pw**eh**do bair]
  I'm just looking sólo estoy mirando
  will you look after my bags? ¿me vigilas las
  bolsas? [meh bee**Hee**lass...]
  I'm looking for... estoy buscando...
  look out! ¡cuidado! [kweed**ah**do]
loose suelto [sw**e**lto]
lorry un camión [kam-y**o**n]
lorry driver un camionero [kam-yon**eh**-ro]
lose perder [paird**air**]
  I've lost... he perdido... [eh paird**ee**do]
  excuse me, I'm lost oiga, por favor, me he
  perdido [**oy**-ga...]
lost property (office) la oficina de objetos
  perdidos [ofee-th**ee**na deh ob-H**eh**-toss
  paird**ee**doss]
lot: a lot mucho [m**oo**tcho]
  not a lot no mucho
  a lot of chips muchas patatas
  a lot of wine mucho vino
  a lot more expensive mucho más caro
lotion una loción [loth-y**o**n]
loud (noise) fuerte [fw**air**teh]
  it's too loud está demasiado fuerte [...deh-
  mass-y**ah**do...]
  louder más fuerte
lounge (in house, hotel) el salón
  (at airport) la sala de espera [...esp**eh**-ra]
love: I love you te quiero [teh kee-**eh**-ro]
  do you love me? ¿me quieres? [meh kee-**eh**-
  ress]
  he's/she's in love está enamorado/a [-**ah**do/a]

I love this wine me encanta este vino
lovely encantad*o*r
(view etc) precioso [preth-y*o*so]
(meal etc) buenísimo [bweh-n*ee*seemo]
low bajo [b*ah*-но]
luck la suerte [sw*air*-teh]
good luck! ¡suerte!
lucky: you're lucky tiene suerte [tee-*eh*-neh sw*air*-teh]
that's lucky! ¡qué suerte! [keh…]
luggage el equipaje [ekeep*ah*-неh]
lunch el almuerzo [al-mw*air*-tho]

✈ Lunch is normally available 1.30-3.30pm.

lungs los pulmones [pool-m*o*-ness]
luxury el lujo [l*oo*-но]

M [*eh*-meh]

mad loco
made-to-measure hecho a la medida [*e*tcho ah la med*ee*da]
magazine una revista [reb*ee*sta]
magnificent magnífico
maid la camarera [kama-r*eh*-ra]
maiden name el nombre de soltera [n*o*mbreh deh sol-t*eh*-ra]

✈ Spanish women keep their maiden name even when married.

mail el correo [kor*eh*-o]
is there any mail for me? ¿hay correo para mí? [ı…]
main road la calle principal [k*a*-yeh preentheep*a*l]
(in the country) la carretera principal [karet*eh*-ra…]
make hacer [ath*air*]

will we make it in time? ¿llegaremos a tiempo? [yeh-gar**eh**-moss ah tee-**e**mpo]
make-up el maquillaje [makee-y**ah**-Heh]
man un hombre [**o**mbreh]
manager el encarg**a**do
 (woman) la encarg**a**da
 (of bank, hotel) el director [deerekt**o**r]
 (woman) la direct**o**ra
 can I see the manager? quiero ver al encargado [kee-**eh**-ro bair…]
many muchos [m**oo**tchoss]
map un mapa
March marzo [m**a**rtho]
marina el puerto deportivo [pw**ai**rto deport**ee**bo]
market el mercado [mairk**ah**do]
marmalade la mermelada de naranja [mairmeh-l**ah**-da deh nar**a**n-Ha]
married casado [kas**ah**do]
marry: will you marry me? ¿te quieres *casar* conmigo? [teh kee-**eh**-ress kas**a**r konme**e**go]
marvellous maravilloso [-bee-y**o**-so]
mascara el rímel
mashed potatoes el puré de patatas [poor**eh**…]
mass *(in church)* la misa [m**ee**sa]
massage un masaje [mass**ah**-Heh]
mast el mástil
mat una estera [est**eh**ra]
match: a box of matches una caja de *cerillas* [k**ah**-Hah deh ther**ee**-yass]
 a football match un partido de fútbol [part**ee**do…]
material *(cloth)* el tejido [teh-H**ee**do]
matter: it doesn't matter no importa
 what's the matter? ¿qué pasa? [keh…]
mattress un colchón
mature maduro [-d**oo**-]
maximum máximo

May mayo [**m**ah-yo]
may: may I have...? ¿me da...? [meh...]
maybe tal vez [...beth]
mayonnaise la mayonesa [mah-yon**eh**-sa]
me: he knows me me conoce [meh kon**o**theh]
  can you send it to me? ¿me lo puede
  mandar? [...pw**eh**deh...]
  it's for me es para mí [...mee]
  it's me soy yo
  who? – me ¿quién? – yo
meal una comida [kom**ee**da]
mean: what does this mean? ¿qué significa
  esto? [keh seegneef**ee**ka...]
measles el sarampión [-yon]
  German measles la rubéola [roob**eh**-ola]
measurements las medidas [-d**ee**-]
meat la carne [k**a**rneh]
mechanic: is there a mechanic here? ¿hay
  algún mecánico aquí? [ɪ...ak**ee**]
medicine *(for cold etc)* una medicina [-th**ee**na]
Mediterranean el Mediterráneo [mehdee-teh-
  r**a**-neh-o]
meet encontrar
  pleased to meet you mucho gusto (en
  conocerle) [m**oo**tcho g**oo**sto (en konoth**air**-
  leh)]
  I met him in the street me encontré con él
  en la calle [meh enkontr**eh**...k**a**h-yeh]
  when shall we meet? ¿cuándo nos reunimos?
  [kw**a**ndo noss reh-oon**ee**moss]
meeting una reunión [reh-oon-y**on**]
melon un melón
member un/una socio [s**oth**-yo]
  how do I become a member? ¿cómo puedo
  hacerme socio? [...pw**eh**do ath**air**-meh...]
men los hombres [**o**mbress]
mend: can you mend this? ¿puede arregl**a**r

esto? [pw**eh**deh…]

men's room los aseos [ass**eh**-oss]

mention: don't mention it de nada [deh…]

menu el menú [men**oo**]

  can I have the menu, please? ¿me trae el menú, por fav**o**r? [meh tr**ah**-eh…]

✈ Look for the **menú del día** for cheaper set daily menus.

go to pages 82-85

mess un lío [l**ee**-o]

message un recado [reh-k**ah**do]

  (text) un mensaje [mensa**н**eh]

  are there any messages for me? ¿hay algún recado para mí? [ɪ alg**oo**n…]

  can I leave a message for…? quisiera dejar un recado para… [keess-y**eh**-ra deh-**н**ar…]

metre un metro

✈ 1 metre = 39.37 inches = 1.09 yds

metro underground

  ✈ There's a flat-rate fare; buy a **metrobus** book of tickets for cheaper travel (but tickets will not be valid across the outlying suburban network).

midday: at midday a mediodía [ah mehd-yo-d**ee**-a]

middle: in the middle en el centro [th-]

  in the middle of the road en medio de la calle [en m**eh**d-yo deh la k**ah**-yeh]

midnight medianoche [mehd-ya-n**o**tcheh]

might: he might have gone es posible que se haya ido […pos**ee**bleh keh seh **ah**-yah **ee**do]

migraine una jaqueca [**н**ak**eh**-ka]

mild suave [sw**ah**-beh]

  (weather) templ**a**do

I'd like
quisiera
[keess-y**eh**-ra]

Entradas: Starters

aceitunas rellenas stuffed olives
boquerones en vinagre anchovies
in vinaigrette
cóctel de gambas prawn cocktail
ensalada mixta mixed salad
ensaladilla rusa Russian salad
entremeses variados assorted hors
d'oeuvres
jamón serrano cured ham
pimientos rellenos stuffed peppers
setas a la plancha grilled
mushrooms

Sopas: Soups

sopa del día soup of the day
caldo de pescado clear fish soup
consomé de pollo chicken
consommé
crema de espárragos cream of
asparagus soup
gazpacho andaluz cold soup made
from tomatoes, onions, garlic,
peppers and cucumber
sopa de pescado fish soup

Pescado y Mariscos: Fish & Shellfish

almejas en salsa verde clams in
parsley and white wine sauce
bacalao al pil pil cod cooked in
olive oil
besugo al horno baked sea bream
boquerones fritos fried fresh
anchovies
calamares en su tinta squid cooked
in their ink
calamares fritos fried squid

water
agua

bread
pan

chipirones rellenos stuffed baby squid

gambas al ajillo prawns with garlic

langosta a la catalana lobster with mushrooms and ham in a white sauce

lenguado a la plancha grilled sole

mejillones a la marinera mussels in a wine sauce with garlic and parsley

merluza a la romana hake steaks in batter

paella valenciana paella with shellfish and chicken

pescaditos fritos whitebait

pez espada ahumado smoked swordfish

rape a la plancha grilled monkfish

sardinas a la brasa barbecued sardines

truchas molinera trout coated in flour, fried and served with butter, lemon juice and parsley

zarzuela de mariscos shellfish stew

Carnes y Guisados: Meat Dishes and Stews

champiñones al ajillo mushrooms fried with garlic

chuletas de cerdo pork chops

cocido stew with meat, chickpeas and vegetables

escalope a la milanesa breaded veal escalope with cheese

filete de ternera veal steak

guisado de cordero stewed lamb

hígado de ternera estofado braised calves' liver

red wine
vino tinto

white wine
vino blanco

beer
cerveza
[thair-**beh**-tha]

can I have what he's having?
póngame lo mismo que tiene él
[...tee-**eh**-neh]

beef
carne de vaca

chicken
pollo

lamb
cordero

> **very nice**
> muy bueno
> [mwee
> bwehno]

habas con jamón broad beans with ham and egg
pechuga de pollo chicken breast
pinchos morunos kebabs
pollo al ajillo fried chicken with garlic
pollo asado roast chicken
potaje de garbanzos chickpea stew
riñones al jerez kidneys in a sherry sauce
solomillo de cerdo fillet of pork

Verduras: Vegetables

coles de Bruselas Brussels sprouts
coliflor cauliflower
espárragos asparagus
habas fritas fried young broad beans
judías verdes green beans
patatas cocidas boiled potatoes
patatas fritas French fries (*also* crisps)
pisto fried peppers, onions, tomatoes and courgettes
puré de patata potato purée, mashed potatoes

> **coffee**
> un café
> [kafeh]

Huevos: Egg dishes

arroz a la cubana boiled rice with fried eggs and either bananas or tomato sauce
huevos a la flamenca baked eggs with sausage, tomato, peas, asparagus and peppers
huevos fritos con chorizo fried eggs with spicy Spanish sausage
tortilla española (cold) Spanish omelette with potato, onion and garlic

Postres y Fruta: Desserts and Fruit

arroz con leche rice pudding
ensalada de frutas fruit salad
flan crème caramel
fresas con nata strawberries and cream
fruta variada assorted fresh fruit
helado ice cream
macedonia de fruta fruit salad
melocotones en almíbar peaches in syrup
melón melon
natillas cold custard with cinnamon
piña pineapple
plátano banana
queso de Burgos soft white cheese
queso manchego hard, strong cheese from La Mancha
sandía water melon
tarta de almendra almond tart or gâteau
tarta helada ice cream gâteau
uvas grapes

General terms:

bien hecho well done
incluye pan, postre y vino includes bread, dessert and wine
IVA no incluido VAT not included
menú del día today's set menu
platos combinados meat and vegetables, hamburgers and eggs etc, various foods served as one dish
poco hecho rare
ración pequeña para niños children's portion

vanilla
de vainilla
[deh bI-**nee**ya]

strawberry
de fresa
[deh fr**eh**-sa]

chocolate
de chocolate
[deh choko-**lah**-teh]

the bill, please
la cuenta, por fav**o**r

mile una milla [m**ee**-ya]

> ✈ miles/5 x 8 = kilometres
>
> | miles | 0.5 | 1 | 3 | 5 | 10 | 50 | 100 |
> |---|---|---|---|---|---|---|---|
> | kilometres | 0.8 | 1.6 | 4.8 | 8 | 16 | 80 | 160 |

milk la leche [l**eh**-cheh]
  a glass of milk un vaso de leche [b**ah**-so deh...]

> ✈ UHT milk is more common than fresh.

milkshake un batido [-t**ee**-]
millimetre un milímetro
milometer el cuentakilómetros [kwenta-]
mind: I've changed my mind he cambiado de idea [eh kamb-y**ah**do deh eed**eh**-a]
  I don't mind me es igual [meh es eeg-w**al**]
  do you mind if I...? ¿le importa si...? [leh...]
  never mind ¡qué más da! [keh...]
mine mío/mía [m**ee**-o...]
mineral water un agua mineral [**ah**g-wa meeneh-r**al**]
minimum mínimo
minus menos [m**eh**-noss]
  minus 3 degrees tres grados bajo cero [...b**ah**-нo th**eh**-ro]
minute un minuto [-een**oo**-]
  in a minute en seguida [en seg**ee**-da]
  just a minute un momento
mirror un espejo [esp**eh**-нo]
Miss Señorita [sen-yor**ee**ta]
miss: I miss you te echo de menos [teh **e**tcho deh m**eh**-noss]
  he's missing falta
  there is a...missing falta un/una...
  we missed the bus hemos perdido el autobús [**eh**-moss paird**ee**do...]
mist la bruma [br**oo**ma]
mistake una equivocación [ekeebo-kath-y**on**]

I think you've made a mistake me parece que se ha equivocado [meh par**eh**-theh keh seh ah ekeebok**ah**do]

misunderstanding un malentend**i**do

mobile (phone) un (teléfono) móvil [...mo-beel]

  my mobile number is... mi número de móvil es el... [mee n**oo**-...]

modern moderno [-d**air**-]

moisturizer una crema hidratante [kr**eh**ma eedrat**a**nteh]

Monday lunes [l**oo**ness]

money el dinero [dee-n**eh**-ro]

  I've lost my money se me ha perdido el dinero [seh meh ah pairde**e**do...]

  I have no money no tengo dinero

money belt una riñonera [reen-yon**eh**-ra]

month un mes [mehss]

moon la luna [l**oo**na]

moorings el amarradero [-d**eh**ro]

moped un ciclomotor [theeklo-]

more más

  can I have some more? ¿me da un poco más? [meh...]

  more wine, please más vino, por fav**o**r

  no more ya no más

  no more thanks ya vale, gracias [...b**ah**-leh-...]

  more than that más que eso [...keh...]

  I haven't got any more ya no tengo más

  more comfortable más cómodo

morning la mañana [man-y**ah**-na]

  good morning buenos días [bw**eh**-noss d**ee**-ass]

  in the morning por la mañana

  (tomorrow) mañana por la mañana

  this morning esta mañana

mosquito un mosquito

most: I like this one the most es el que *más* me

gusta [...keh...]

most of the people la mayoría de la gente [ma-yor**ee**-a...н**e**nteh]

mother: my mother mi madre [mee m**ah**-dreh]

motor el mot**o**r

motorbike una moto

motorboat una mot**o**ra

motorcyclist un/una motorista [-**ree**-]

motorist un/una automovilista [owto-mobee**lee**sta]

motorway la autopista [owto-p**ee**sta]

> ✈ You have to pay a toll on some motorways north of Madrid.

mountain una montaña [mont**ah**n-ya]

mouse *(also for computer)* un ratón

moustache el bigote [beeg**o**teh]

mouth la boca

move: don't move no se mueva [no seh mw**eh**-ba]

could you move your car? ¿podría cambiar de sitio su coche? [podr**ee**-a kamb-y**a**r deh s**ee**t-yo soo k**o**tcheh]

movie una película [peh-l**ee**-koola]

MPV un monovolumen [-bol**oo**men]

Mr Señor [sen-y**o**r]

Mrs Señora [sen-y**o**ra]

Ms Señora [sen-y**o**ra]

much mucho [m**oo**tcho]

much better mucho mejor [...meh-н**o**r]

not much no mucho

mug: I've been mugged me han atacado [meh an atak**ah**do]

mum mamá

muscle un músculo [m**oo**skoolo]

museum el museo [moos**eh**-o]

✈ Most museums, castles and monuments close on Sunday afternoons and Mondays, although main attractions open every day, especially during the high season.

mushrooms unos champiñones [champeen-yo-ness]

music la música [m**oo**sseeka]

must: I must… tengo que… [t**e**ng-go keh]

I must not eat… no debo comer… [no d**eh**bo kom**air**]

you must do it debe de hacerlo [d**eh**-beh deh ath**air**-lo]

must I…? ¿tengo que…?

you mustn't… no debes…

mustard la mostaza [most**ah**-tha]

my mi [mee]

No feminine ending; plural is **mis**.

N [**eh**-neh]

nail *(on finger)* una uña [**oo**n-ya]

(for wood) un clavo [kl**ah**-vo]

nail clippers un cortauñas [korta-**oo**n-yass]

nail file una lima para las uñas [l**ee**ma…**oo**n-yass]

nail polish el esmalte para las uñas [esm**a**lteh…**oo**n-yass]

nail scissors unas tijeritas de uñas [tee-нeh-r**ee**tass deh **oo**n-yass]

naked desnudo [dess-n**oo**do]

name el nombre [n**o**mbreh]

my name is… me llamo… [meh y**ah**-mo]

what's your name? ¿cómo te llamas? […teh y**ah**-mass]

napkin una servilleta [sairbee-y**eh**-ta]

nappy un pañal [pan-y**al**]

narrow estrecho

national nacional [nath-yon**a**l]

nationality la nacionalidad [nath-yonaleed**a**]

natural natural [na-too-r**a**l]

naughty: don't be naughty ¡no seas malo!
  [...s**eh**-ass...]

near: is it near? ¿está cerca? [...th**air**ka]
  near here cerca de aquí [...deh ak**ee**]
  do you go near...? ¿va a pas**a**r cerca de...?
  where's the nearest...? ¿dónde está el/la...más
  cercano/a? [...thair-k**ah**-no]

nearly casi [k**a**h-see]

neat *(drink)* solo

necessary necesario [nethess**a**r-yo]
  it's not necessary no es necesario

neck el cuello [kw**eh**-yo]

necklace un collar [koy-y**a**r]

need: I need a... necesito un... [nethess**ee**to...]

needle una aguja [ag**oo**-на]

neighbour el vecino [beth**ee**no]
  (woman) la vecina

neither: neither of them ninguno/a de los/las
  dos [neeng**oo**no/a...]
  neither...nor... ni...ni... [nee...]
  neither do I ni yo tamp**o**co

nephew: my nephew mi sobrino [mee sobr**ee**no]

nervous nervioso [nairbee-**o**so]

net *(fishing)* una red [reth]

never nunca [n**oo**nka]

new nuevo [nw**eh**-bo]

news las noticias [no-t**ee**th-yass]

> ✈ Main news on TV is at 2.30/3pm and 8.30/
> 9pm.

newsagent's una tienda de periódicos [tee-y**e**n-
  da deh peh-ree-**o**deekoss]

newspaper un periódico [peh-ree-**o**deeko]

do you have any English newspapers? ¿tiene
algún periódico inglés? [tee-**eh**-neh alg**oo**n…
eengl**ess**]

✈ British newspapers are often available in
kioskos in the city centre.

New Year el Año Nuevo [an-yo nw**eh**-bo]
Happy New Year Feliz Año Nuevo [fehl**ee**th….]

✈ In Spain it is traditional to swallow one
grape on each stroke of midnight for good
luck.

New Year's Eve Nochevieja [n**o**tcheh-bee-**eh**-нa]
New Zealand Nueva Zelanda [nw**eh**-ba theh-
l**a**nda]
next próximo
  please stop at the next corner pare en la
  esquina próxima, por favor [p**a**reh…esk**ee**na…]
  see you next year hasta el año que viene [**a**sta
  el **a**n-yo keh bee-**eh**-neh]
  next week/next Tuesday la semana/el martes
  que viene
  next to the hotel al lado del hotel […l**ah**do…]
next of kin el pariente más próximo [par**ee**-
  enteh…]
nice agradable [-d**ah**-bleh]
  (nice-looking) guapo [gw**ah**po]
niece: my niece mi sobrina [mee sobr**ee**na]
night la noche [n**o**tcheh]
  good night buenas noches [bw**eh**-nass
  n**o**tchess]
  at night por la noche
night club un cabaret [-r**eh**]
nightdress un camisón
night porter el portero [port**eh**-ro]
no no
  there's no water no hay agua [no ı **ah**g-wa]

I've no money no tengo dinero

no potable not for drinking

nobody nadie [n**ah**d-yeh]

noisy ruidoso [rweed**o**so]
  our room is too noisy se oye demasiado ruido en nuestra habitación [seh **o**-yeh demass-y**ah**do rw**ee**-do en nw**e**stra abee-tath-y**o**n]

none ninguno [neeng**oo**no]
  none of them ninguno de ellos [...deh **eh**-yoss]

non-smoker: we're non-smokers no somos fumadores [...foomad**o**ress]

nor: nor am/do I ni yo tamp**o**co

normal norm**a**l

north el norte [n**o**rteh]

Northern Ireland Irlanda del Norte [eerl**a**nda del n**o**rteh]

nose la nariz [-**ee**th]

not no
  not that one ése no [**eh**-seh...]
  not me yo no
  I'm not hungry no tengo hambre [...**a**mbreh]
  he didn't tell me no me lo dijo [...meh lo d**ee**-Ho]

note (bank note) un billete [bee-y**eh**-teh]

nothing nada [n**ah**da]

November noviembre [nobee-**e**mbreh]

now ahora [ah-**o**ra]

nowhere en ningún sitio [en neeng**oo**n s**ee**t-yo]

nudist beach una playa nudista [pl**ah**-ya nood**ee**sta]

nuisance: it's a nuisance es una lata
  this man's being a nuisance este hombre me está molestando [...**o**mbreh meh...]

numb estumecido [estoomeh-th**ee**do]

number (figure) un número [n**oo**-]

number plate la placa de matrícula [... matr**ee**koola]

nurse un/una ATS [ah-teh-**eh**-seh]
nut una nuez [nweth]
  (for bolt) una tuerca [tw**air**ka]

O [oh]

oar un remo [r**eh**-mo]
objetos perdidos lost property
obligatory obligatorio [obleegat**o**r-yo]
obras roadworks
obviously evidentemente [-m**e**nteh]
occasionally de vez en cuando [deh beth en
  kw**a**ndo]
o'clock *go to* **time**
October octubre [okt**oo**breh]
octopus un pulpo [p**oo**lpo]
ocupado engaged
odd *(number)* impar [eem-p**a**r]
  (strange) raro [r**ah**-ro]
of de [deh]

> **De**, when used with **el** changes to **del**.
>   **the name of the hotel** el nombre del
>   hotel

off: the milk is off la leche está cortada […
  kort**ah**da]
  the meat is off la carne está pasada […
  k**a**rneh…pas**ah**da]
  it just came off se ha soltado sin más [seh ah…]
  10% off un descuento del diez por ciento [oon
  dess-kw**e**nto del dee-**e**th por thee-**e**nto]
office la oficina [ofeeth**ee**na]
official un funcionario [foonth-yon**ah**-ree-o]
  (woman) una funcionaria
often a menudo [ah men**oo**do]
  how often? ¿cada cuánto tiempo? […tee-**e**mpo]
  not often pocas veces [p**o**-kass b**eh**-thess]

how often do the buses go? ¿cada cuánto
pasan los autobuses? [...kw**a**nto...owto-b**oo**sess]

> YOU MAY THEN HEAR
> cada diez minutos *every ten minutes*
> dos veces al día *twice a day*

oil el aceite [ath**a**y-teh]
  will you change the oil? ¿quiere cambiar el
  aceite? [kee-**e**h-reh kamb-y**a**r...]
ointment una pom**a**da
ok ¡vale! [b**a**h-leh]
  it's ok *(doesn't matter)* no importa
  are you ok? ¿estás bien? [...bee-**e**n]
  that's ok by me por mí vale [...mee...]
  is this ok for the airport? *(bus, train)* ¿va al
  aeropuerto? [ba...]
  more wine? – no, I'm ok thanks ¿un poco
  más de vino? – no, gracias, no me apetece más
  [...no meh apet**e**h-theh...]
old viejo [bee-**e**h-нo]
  how old are you? ¿cuántos años tienes?
  [kw**a**ntoss an-yoss tee-**e**h-ness]

> **I am 28** tengo ventiocho [t**e**ng-go...]

olive una aceituna [athay-t**oo**na]
olive oil el aceite de oliva [ath**a**y-teh deh ol**ee**ba]
omelette una tortilla [tort**ee**ya]
on en
  I haven't got it on me no lo llevo encima
  [...y**e**h-bo enth**ee**ma]
  on Friday el viernes [bee-**air**ness]
  on television en la tele [...t**e**h-leh]
once una vez [beth]
  at once *(immediately)* en seguida [seh-g**ee**da]
one uno/una [**oo**no...]
  (number) uno
  the red one el rojo/la roja [r**o**-нo...]

onion una cebolla [theh-b**o**y-ya]
on-line: to pay on-line pag**a**r por Internet
[…eentairn**e**t]
only sólo
  the only one el único/la única [**oo**neeko…]
open *(adjective)* abierto [abee-**air**to]
  I can't open it no puedo abrirlo [no pw**eh**do
  abr**ee**rlo]
   when do you open? ¿a qué hora abre? [ah keh
   ora **ah**-breh]
open ticket un billete abierto [beey**eh**-teh abee-
  airto]
opera la ópera
operation una operación [-ath-y**o**n]
operator *(telephone)* la operad**o**ra
opposite: opposite the hotel enfrente del hotel
  [emfr**e**nteh del o-t**e**l]
optician's una óptica
or o
orange *(fruit)* una naranja [nar**a**n-нa]
  (colour) naranja
orange juice un zumo de naranja [th**oo**mo deh
  nar**a**n-нa]
order: could we order now? ¿podemos *pedir* ya
  la comida? [pod**eh**-moss ped**ee**r ya la kom**ee**da]
  thank you, we've already ordered gracias, ya
  hemos pedido […ya **eh**-moss ped**ee**do]
other: the other one el otro/la otra
  do you have any others? ¿tiene otros
  distintos? [tee-**eh**-neh…]
otherwise si no
ought: I ought to go *debería* irme [deber**ee**-a
  eer-meh]
our nuestro/nuestra [nw**e**stro…]
  (plural) nuestros/nuestras
ours: that's ours eso es nuestro/nuestra […
  nw**e**stro…]

out: we're out of petrol se nos ha acabado la
  gasolina [seh noss ha akab**ah**do...]
  get out! ¡fuera! [fw**eh**-ra]
outboard un mot**o**r fuerabordo [...fw**eh**-ra-]
outdoors fuera de casa [fw**eh**-ra...]
outside: can we sit outside? ¿podemos
  sentarnos fuera? [pod**eh**-moss...fw**eh**-ra]
over: over here aquí [ak**ee**]
  over there allá [ah-y**a**]
  over 40 más de cuarenta [...deh...]
  it's all over (finished) se acabó [seh...]
overcharge: you've overcharged me me ha
  cobrado de más [meh ah...]
overcooked recocido [reh-koth**ee**do]
overexposed sobreexpuesto [so-breh-espw**e**sto]
overnight (travel) durante la noche [doo-r**a**nteh la
  n**o**tcheh]
oversleep: I overslept se me han peg**a**do las
  sábanas [seh meh an...]
overtake adelant**a**r
owe: what do I owe you? ¿cuánto le *debo*?
  [kw**a**nto leh d**eh**-bo]
own: my own... mi pr**o**pio/a...
  I'm on my own estoy solo/a
owner el propietario [pro-pee-eh-t**a**r-yo]
  (female) la propietaria
oxygen el oxígeno [ox**ee**-Heh-no]
oysters unas ostras

P [peh]

pack: I haven't packed yet todavía no he
  hecho las maletas [todab**ee**-a no eh **e**tcho lass
  mal**eh**tass]
  can I have a packed lunch? ¿me puede poner
  la comida en bocadillos? [meh pw**eh**deh pon**air**
  la kom**ee**da en bokad**ee**-yoss]

package tour un viaje organizado [bee-**ah**-Heh organeeth**ah**do]

page (of book) la página [p**ah**-Heena]

    could you page him? ¿podría llamarle por los altavoces? [podr**ee**-a yam**a**rleh por loss altab**o**thess]

pain el dol**o**r

    I've got a pain in my... me duele el/la... [meh dw**eh**-leh...]

painkillers unos analgésicos [analH**eh**-seekoss]

painting (picture) un cuadro [kw**a**dro]

Pakistan Paquistán

pale pálido

pancake una crêpe [krep]

panties las bragas

pants los pantalones [-**o**-ness]

    (underpants) los calzoncillos [kalthon-th**ee**yoss]

paper el pap**e**l

    (newspaper) un periódico [peh-ree-**o**deeko]

parada stop (bus etc)

parcel un paquete [pak**eh**-teh]

pardon? (didn't understand) ¿cómo?

    I beg your pardon (sorry) usted perdone [oost**eh** pairdoneh]

parents: my parents mis padres [meess p**ah**-dress]

park el parque [p**a**rkeh]

    where can I park my car? ¿dónde puedo aparc**a**r el coche? [d**o**ndeh pw**e**hdo...]

    is it difficult to get parked? ¿es difícil encontr**a**r aparcamiento? [...aparkam-y**e**nto]

> ✈ You have to pay in **zona azul** areas (blue lined zones) and display the ticket on your windscreen. Maximum stay is usually 2 hours.

parking ticket una multa (por estacionamiento indebido) [...estath-yonam-y**e**nto eendeb**ee**do]

part una parte [p**a**rteh]
  a (spare) part una pieza de repuesto [pee-**eh**-tha deh repw**e**sto]
partner *(male)* el compañero [kompan-y**eh**-ro]
  (female) la compañera
party *(group)* el grupo [gr**oo**po]
  (celebration) una fiesta
  I'm with the...party estoy en el grupo de...
pasen cross
paso a nivel level crossing
pass *(in mountains)* el puerto [pw**air**to]
  he's passed out ha perdido el conocimiento
  [ah pairdeedo el konotheem-yento]
passable *(road)* transitable [-eet**ah**-bleh]
passenger un pasajero [passa-нeh-ro]
  (female) una pasajera
passer-by un/una transeúnte [tran-seh-**oo**nteh]
passport el pasaporte [passap**o**rteh]
past: in the past antiguamente
  [anteegwam**e**nteh]
  it's just past the traffic lights está justo
  después de los semáforos [...нoosto despw**e**ss
  deh...]
  go to **time**
path el camino [-m**ee**-]
patient: be patient tenga paciencia [...path-
  y**e**nth-ya]
pattern el dibujo [dee-b**oo**-нo]
pavement la acera [ath**e**h-ra]
pavement café una terraza [ter**a**tha]
pay pag**a**r
  can I pay, please ¿me puede cobr**a**r, por fav**o**r?
  [meh pw**eh**deh...]

  ✈ It is usual to pay when you leave not when
    you order.

peace la paz [path]

peach un melocotón [mehlo-koton]
peaje toll
peanuts unos cacahuetes [kaka-weh-tess]
pear una pera [peh-ra]
peas unos guisantes [gee-santess]
peatones pedestrians
pedestrian un peatón [peh-ah-ton]
pedestrian crossing un paso de peatones […
   peh-ah-toness]

> ✈ Beware! Cars do not usually stop unless you
>   brave it across.

peg (for washing) una pinza [peen-tha]
   (for tent) una estaca
peligro danger
peligro de incendio danger of fire
pen un bolígrafo [boleegrafo]
pencil un lápiz [lapeeth]
penicillin la penicilina [peneetheeleena]
penknife una navaja [nabah-на]
pensioner un/una pensionista [penss-yoneesta]
people la gente [Henteh]
   how many people? ¿cuántas personas?
   [kwantass pair-sonass]
people carrier un monovolumen [-boloomen]
pepper la pimienta [peem-yenta]
   green/red pepper un pimiento verde/morrón
   […bairdeh]
peppermint (sweet, flavour) la menta
per: per night/person por noche/persona
per cent por ciento […thee-ento]
perfect perfecto [pair-]
perfume el perfume [pairfoomeh]
perhaps quizás [keethass]
period (of time, woman) el período [peh-ree-odo]
permit un permiso [pair-meeso]
person una persona [pair-sona]

in person en persona
personal stereo un walkman®
petrol la gasolina [-**ee**na]
petrol station una gasolinera [-een**eh**-ra]

✈ Mostly self-service but still some with pump
   attendant.

YOU MAY SEE
Ecosuper97 sin plomo = 4-star unleaded
   but with lead substitute for cars that
   can't use unleaded
Eurosuper95 sin plomo = unleaded 95
Eurosuper98 sin plomo = unleaded 98
Gasoil/Gasoleo A = diesel
Mezcla = oil and diesel mix for motorbikes

---

pharmacy una farmacia [farm**a**th-ya]

✈ *go to* **chemist**

phone el teléfono [tel**e**fono]
I'll phone you le/la llamaré [leh/la yamar**eh**]
(familiar) te llamaré
I'll phone you back ya te llamaré
can you phone back in five minutes? ¿puedes
volver a llamar dentro de cinco minutos?
[pw**eh**dess bolb**air**…]

---

can I speak to…? ¿se puede poner…? [seh
pw**eh**deh pon**air**]
could you get the number for me?
¿podría marcarme el número? [podr**ee**-a
mark**a**r-meh el n**oo**meh-ro]

YOU MAY HEAR
en este momento no podemos atender a
   su llamada; deje su mensaje después del
   tono *we're unable to come to the phone*

> right now; please leave a message after the
> tone
> por favor, manténgase a la espera – o
> vuelva a llamar más tarde *please hold the
> line – or call back later*

> *YOU MAY SEE*
> introduzca la tarjeta/las monedas *insert
> your card/coins*
> marque el número *dial number*

phonebox una cabina telefónica

✈ Money or phonecard; phonecards can be
bought in tobacconists and kiosks and
are often better value for money; put in
first, then dial; unused coins will NOT be
returned; for UK dial 0044 then dial the
number; omit first 0 of UK area code.

phonecall una llamada [yam**ah**da]
 can I make a phonecall? ¿puedo llamar por
 teléfono? [pw**eh**do yam**ar**...]
phonecard una tarjeta telefónica [tarн**eh**-ta...]
photograph una foto
 would you take a photograph of us/me?
 ¿le importaría hacernos/hacerme una foto?
 [leh eemportar**ee**-ah ath**air**-noss/ath**air**-meh...]
piano un piano
pickpocket un ratero [rat**eh**ro]
picture *(painting)* un cuadro [kw-]
pie *(meat)* una empanada
 (fruit) una tarta
piece un pedazo [ped**ah**-tho]
 a piece of... un pedazo de...
pig un cerdo [th**air**do]
pigeon una pal**o**ma
pile-up un accidente múltiple [ak-theed**e**nteh

m**oo**lteepleh]

pill una píldora [p**ee**ldora]
  are you on the pill? ¿tomas la píldora?
pillow una almohada [almo-**ah**-da]
pin un alfiler [alfee-l**air**]
pineapple una piña [p**ee**n-ya]
pink rosa
pint una pinta [p**ee**nta]

✈ 1 pint = 0.57 litres

pipe *(to smoke)* una pipa [p**ee**pa]
  (for water) el tubo [t**oo**bo]
piso floor; apartment
pity: it's a pity es una lástima
place un sitio [s**ee**t-yo]
  is this place taken? ¿está ocupado este sitio?
  do you know any good places to go? ¿sabe
  de sitios buenos adonde ir? [s**ah**-beh…bw**eh**-
  noss ad**o**ndeh eer]
  at my place en mi casa
  at your place en tu casa
  to your place a tu casa
plain sencillo [sen-th**ee**yo]
  (not patterned) liso [l**ee**so]
  a plain omelette una tortilla francesa [tort**ee**ya
  fran-th**eh**-sa]
plane el avión [ab-y**o**n]
plant una planta
planta floor
planta baja ground floor
plaster *(cast)* una escayola [eska-y**o**la]
  (sticking) una tirita [teer**ee**ta]
plastic plástico
plastic bag una bolsa de plástico
plate un plato
platform *(station)* el andén
  which platform please? ¿qué andén, por

favor? [keh...]
play jugar [Hoog**a**r]
pleasant agradable [-d**ah**-bleh]
please por favor [por fa-b**o**r]
 could you please...? ¿podría...?
 [podr**ee**-a...]
 (yes) please sí, gracias [gr**a**th-yass]

> **Por favor** is not used as much as 'please'
> is in English.

pleasure el placer [plath**air**]
 it's a pleasure no hay de qué [no ɪ deh keh]
plenty: plenty of... mucho... [m**oo**tcho]
 thank you, that's plenty ya basta, gracias
pliers unos alicates [-**ah**-tess]
plug *(electrical)* un enchufe [ench**oo**feh]
 (for car) una bujía [boo-H**ee**-a]
 (for sink) el tapón

> ✈ 2-pin plugs are used in Spain so buy an
>   adaptor before you go.

plum una ciruela [theer-w**eh**-la]
plumber el fontanero [-**eh**ro]
plus más
pm de la tarde [...t**a**rdeh]

> ✈ Official times are expressed by the 24hr
>   system.

pocket un bolsillo [bols**ee**-yo]
point: could you point to it? ¿puede señalarlo?
 [pw**eh**deh senyal**a**rlo]
 4 point 6 4 coma 6 [kw**a**tro k**o**ma sayss]
police la policía [polee-th**ee**-a]
 get the police llame a la policía [y**ah**-meh...]

> ✈ Three types of police in Spain: **la policía
>   local** (local police, navy blue uniform) who

take care of the traffic in towns and cities and are run by the town/city council – dial 092 for emergencies; **la guardia civil** (civil guard, green uniform), a remnant of the dictatorship who basically take care of traffic on main highways – dial 062 for emergencies; and **la policía nacional** (national police, brown uniform) who take care of crime and most other emergencies – dial 091 for emergencies.

policeman un policía [polee-thee-a]
police station la comisaría [-ree-a]
policewoman una mujer policía [mooнair polee-thee-a]
polish el betún [-toon]
  can you polish my shoes? ¿quiere limpiarme los zapatos? [kee-eh-reh leemp-yarmeh loss thapah-toss]

✈ You can have your shoes cleaned in the street by travelling **limpiabotas**.

polite fino [feeno]
polluted contaminado
pool *(swimming)* la piscina [peess-theena]
poor: I'm very poor soy muy pobre […mwee po-breh]
  poor quality de baja calidad [bah-на…]
pork la carne de cerdo [kar-neh deh thairdo]
port un puerto [pwairto]
  (drink) un Oporto
  (not starboard) babor
porter *(in hotel)* el conserje [kon-sair-нeh]
portrait un retrato [retrahto]
Portugal Portugal [-toogal]
Portuguese portugués [-toogess]
posh *(hotel etc)* de lujo [deh loo-нo]

(people) snob [esn**o**b]
possible posible [pos**ee**bleh]
  could you possibly…? ¿le sería posible…? [leh ser**ee**-a…]
post *(mail)* el correo [kor**eh**-o]
postbox un buzón [booth**o**n]
postcard una post**a**l
poste restante la lista de Correos [l**ee**sta deh kor**eh**-oss]
post office la oficina de Correos [ofee-th**ee**na deh kor**eh**-oss]

> ✈ Put letters for abroad in the slot marked **extranjero**; *go to* **stamps**.

potatoes unas patatas [pat**ah**tass]
pound *(money, weight)* una libra [l**ee**bra]

> ✈ pounds/11 x 5 = kilos
>
> | pounds | 1 | 3 | 5 | 6 | 7 | 8 | 9 |
> |--------|------|-----|-----|-----|-----|-----|-----|
> | kilos | 0.45 | 1.4 | 2.3 | 2.7 | 3.2 | 3.6 | 4.1 |

pour: it's pouring está lloviendo a cántaros [yob-y**e**ndo…]
power cut un apagón
power point una toma de corriente […deh kory**e**nteh]
prawns unas gambas
precaución caution
prefer: I prefer this one prefiero éste [pref-y**eh**-ro **e**steh]
  I'd prefer to… prefiero…
  I'd prefer a… preferiría un/una … [prefeh-ree-r**ee**-a…]
pregnant embarazada [embarath**ah**-da]
prescription una receta [reh-th**eh**-ta]
present: at present actualmente [aktwal-m**e**nteh]
  here's a present for you aquí tienes un regalo [ak**ee** tee-**eh**-ness oon reg**ah**-lo]

president el/la presidente [-denteh]
press: could you press these? ¿puede
  planchármelos? [pwehdeh plancharmeh-loss]
pretty mono
  pretty good bastante bueno [bastanteh bweh-
  no]
price el precio [preth-yo]
priest un sacerdote [sathair-doteh]
prioridad a la derecha vehicles coming from the
  right have priority
prison la cárcel [-thel]
private privado [preebahdo]
probably probablemente [probableh-
  menteh]
problem un problema [problehma]
  no problem! no hay problema [...ɪ...]
product un producto [-doo-]
profit la ganancia [gananth-ya]
prohibido forbidden
prohibido adelantar no overtaking
prohibido aparcar no parking
prohibido el paso no trespassing
prohibido fumar no smoking
promise: do you promise? ¿lo promete?
  [...pro-meh-teh]
  I promise lo prometo
pronounce: how do you pronounce this?
  ¿cómo se pronuncia esto? [...seh pronoonth-
  ya...]
propeller una hélice [elee-theh]
properly correctamente [-menteh]
protect proteger [pro-teh-ʜair]
protection factor el factor de protección
  [...deh protekthee-on]
Protestant protestante [-tanteh]
proud orgulloso [orgoo-yoso]
public: the public el público [poo-]

public convenience los aseos públicos [ass-**eh**-oss...]

✈ Public toilets are scarce; *go to* **toilet**.

public holiday un día de fiesta

✈ Jan 1, **Año Nuevo** New Year's Day
Jan 6, **Día de Reyes** Epiphany
Viernes Santo Good Friday
Lunes de Pascua Easter Monday or **Jueves Santo** Good Thursday depending on the region
May 1, **Día del Trabajo** Labour Day
Corpus Christi Corpus Christi
Aug 15, **Día de la Asunción** Assumption
Oct 12, **Día de la Hispanidad** Columbus Day
Nov 1, **Todos los Santos** All Saints Day
Dec 6, **Día de la Constitución** Constitution Day
Dec 8, **Inmaculada Concepción** immaculate Conception
Dec 25, **Navidad** Christmas

pudding un pudín [pood**ee**n]
  (dessert) el postre [p**o**streh]
pull *(verb)* tirar de [teer**a**r deh]
  he pulled out in front of me salió delante de mí sin mirar [sal-y**o** deh-l**a**nteh deh mee seen meer**a**r]
pump la bomba
puncture un pinchazo [peen-ch**a**-tho]
pure puro [p**oo**ro]
purple morado [mor**ah**do]
purse el monedero [-d**eh**ro]
push *(verb)* empujar [empoo-H**a**r]
pushchair una sillita de ruedas [see-y**ee**ta deh rw**eh**-dass]

put: where can I put...? ¿dónde puedo *poner...*?
[d**o**ndeh pw**eh**do pon-**air**]
pyjamas el pijama [pee-н**a**-ma]

Q [koo]

quality la calidad [kaleed**a**]
quarantine la cuarentena [kwarent**eh**-na]
quarter la cuarta parte [kw**a**rta p**a**rteh]
  a quarter of an hour un cuarto de hora [kw**a**rto deh **o**ra]
  go to **time**
quay el muelle [mw**eh**-yeh]
question una pregunta [-g**oo**-]
queue una cola

✈ Don't expect orderly queueing as in the UK.

quick rápido
  that was quick sí que ha sido rápido [see keh ah s**ee**do...]
quiet tranquilo [-k**ee**lo]
  be quiet! ¡cállese! [k**a**-yeh-seh]
quite completamente [kompleta-m**e**nteh]
  (fairly) bastante [bast**a**nteh]
  quite a lot bastante

R [**eh**-reh]

radiator el radiador [radee-ah-d**o**r]
radio la radio [r**a**hd-yo]
rail: by rail en tren
rain la lluvia [y**oo**b-ya]
  it's raining está lloviendo [yob-y**e**ndo]
raincoat un impermeable [eem-pair-meh-**ah**-bleh]
rally *(cars)* el rally
rare poco común [...kom**oo**n]

(steak) poco hecho [...**e**tcho]

raspberry la frambuesa [fram-bw**eh**-sa]

rat una rata

rather: I'd rather have a... preferiría un/una ... [prefeh-ree-r**ee**-a...]

   I'd rather sit here prefiero sentarme aquí [pref-y**eh**-ro sent**a**rmeh ak**ee**]

   I'd rather not prefiero no hacerlo [...ath**ai**r-lo]

   it's rather hot hace *bastante* cal**o**r [**a**theh bast**a**nteh...]

raw crudo [kr**oo**do]

razor *(dry)* una maquinilla de afeitar [makee-n**ee**-ya deh afay-t**a**r]

   (electric) una máquina de afeitar [m**a**keena...]

read: something to read algo para *leer* [...leh-**ai**r]

ready: when will it be ready? ¿cuándo estará listo? [kw**a**ndo estar**a** l**ee**sto]

   I'm not ready yet aún no estoy listo/a [ah-**oo**n...]

real verdadero [bair-da-d**eh**-ro]

really de verdad [deh bair-d**a**]

   (very) muy [mw**ee**]

rear-view mirror el (espejo) retrovisor [(esp**eh**-нo) retro-b**ee**s**o**r]

reasonable razonable [rathon**ah**-bleh]

rebajas sale

receipt un recibo [reth**ee**bo]

   can I have a receipt please? por fav**o**r, ¿me da un recibo?

recently recientemente [reth-yenteh-m**e**nteh]

reception *(hotel)* la recepción [rethepth-y**o**n]

   in reception en recepción

receptionist el/la recepcionista [rethepth-yon**ee**sta]

recién pintado wet paint

recipe una receta [reth**eh**-ta]

recommend: can you recommend…? ¿puede recomendar…? [pweh deh…]

red rojo [ro-Ho]

reduction *(in price)* un descuento [deskwento]

red wine un vino tinto [beeno teento]

refuse: I refuse me niego [meh nee-eh-go]

region la zona [tho-na]

registered: I want to send this registered quiero enviar esto por correo certificado [kee-eh-ro embee-ar…koreh-o thairteefeekahdo]

relax: I just want to relax sólo quiero descansar […kee-eh-ro…]

relax! ¡tranquilo! [tran-keelo]

remember: don't you remember? ¿no te acuerdas? [no teh akwairdass]

I don't remember no recuerdo [no reh-kwairdo]

RENFE = Red Nacional de Ferrocarriles Españoles Spanish National Railways

rent: can I rent a car/bicycle? ¿puedo *alquilar* un coche/una bicicleta? [pwehdo alkeelar oon kotcheh/oona beetheekleh-ta]

YOU MAY HEAR
¿qué tipo? *what type?*
¿para cuántos días? *for how many days?*
kilometraje ilimitado *unlimited mileage*
hay que devolverlo antes de… *you have to bring it back before…*

---

rental car un coche alquilado [kotcheh alkeelahdo]

rep el/la representante comercial [-tanteh komairth-yal]
(activities organizer) el/la representante

repair: can you repair it? ¿puede arreglarlo? [pwehdeh…]

repeat: could you repeat that? ¿puede repetir eso? [pwehdeh reh-peteer…]

reputation la fama [fah-ma]

rescue (verb) rescatar

reservation una reserva [reh-sairba]
  I want to make a reservation for… quiero
  hacer una reserva para… [kee-eh-ro athair…]

reserve: can I reserve a seat? ¿puedo reservar
  un asiento? [pwehdo reh-sairbar oon ass-yento]

> YOU MAY THEN HEAR
> ¿para qué hora? for what time?
> ¿y su nombre es? and your name is?

responsible responsable [-sah-bleh]

rest: I've come here for a rest he venido aquí
  para descansar [eh beneedo akee…]
  you keep the rest quédese con la diferencia
  [keh-deh-seh kon la deeferenth-ya]

restaurant un restaurante [rest-ow-ranteh]

restaurant car el vagón-cafetería [bagon-kafeh-
  teh-ree-a]

retired jubilado [Hoobeelahdo]

retrete toilet

return: a return to… un billete de ida y vuelta
  a… [beeyeh-teh deh eeda ee bwelta…]

reverse charge call una llamada a cobro
  revertido [yamah-da…rebairteedo]

reverse gear la marcha atrás

rheumatism el reúma [reh-ooma]

rib una costilla [kosteeya]

rice el arroz [aroth]

rich (person) rico [reeko]

ridiculous ridículo [reedeekoolo]

right: that's right eso es
  you're right tienes razón [tee-eh-ness rathon]
  on the right a la derecha [dereh-cha]
  right! (understood) ¡bien! [bee-en]

righthand drive con el volante a la derecha
  […bolanteh…]

ring *(on finger)* una sortija [sor-t**ee**-Ha]
ripe maduro [-d**oo**-]
rip-off: it's a rip-off es un timo [...t**ee**mo]
river un río [r**ee**-o]
road la carretera [karet**eh**-ra]
  which is the road to...? ¿cuál es la carretera
  de...? [kwal...]
road map un mapa de carreteras [...deh karet**eh**-
  rass]
rob: I've been robbed me han robado [meh an
  rob**ah**do]
rock una roca
  whisky on the rocks whisky con hielo [...y**eh**-
  lo]
roll *(bread)* un panecillo [paneh-th**ee**yo]
romantic romántico
roof el tejado [teH**ah**do]
roof box una caja portaequipajes [k**a**-Ha porta-
  ekeep**ah**-Hess]
roof rack una baca
room la habitación [abee-tath-y**on**]
  have you got a single/double room? ¿tiene
  una habitación individual/doble? [tee-**eh**-neh...
  eendeebeed-w**al**/d**o**bleh]

---

  for one night para una noche [...n**o**tcheh]
  for three nights para tres noches

YOU MAY THEN HEAR
lo siento, está lleno *sorry, we're full*

---

room service el servicio de habitaciones [sair-
  b**ee**th-yo deh abee-tath-y**o**ness]
rope una cuerda [kw**air**da]
rose una rosa
rough *(sea)* revuelto [reh-bw**el**-to]
roughly *(approx)* aproximadamente [-am**en**teh]
round *(circular)* redondo

it's my round me toca a mí [meh…]
roundabout *(on road)* una rotonda

> ✈ Don't forget to take it anticlockwise. Give
> priority to the car already driving on the
> roundabout, coming from the left.

route una ruta [roota]
  which is the prettiest/fastest route? ¿cuál es
  la ruta más bonita/más rápida? [kwal…]
rowing boat un barco de remos […reh-moss]
rubber la goma
rubber band una goma elástica
rubbish *(waste)* la basura [-soo-]
  (poor quality goods) porquerías [porkeh-ree-ass]
  rubbish! ¡tonterías! [tonteh-ree-ass]
rucksack la mochila [motcheela]
rudder el timón
rude grosero [gro-seh-ro]
ruin una ruina [rweena]
rum un ron
  a rum and coke un cubalibre [koobaleebreh]
run: hurry, run! ¡corre, date prisa! [korreh da-teh
  pree-sa]
  I've run out of petrol/money se me ha
  acabado la gasolina/el dinero [seh meh ah
  akabahdo…]

S [eh-seh]

sad triste [treesteh]
safe seguro [-goo-]
  will it be safe here? ¿estará seguro aquí?
  […akee]
  is it safe to swim here? ¿se puede nadar sin
  peligro aquí? [seh pwehdeh nadar seen peleegro
  akee]
safety la seguridad [segooreeda]

safety pin un imperdible [eem-pair-d**ee**bleh]
sail: can we go sailing? ¿podemos *hacer vela*?
  [pod**eh**-moss ath**air** b**eh**-la]
sailboard un windsurf [ween-s**oo**rf]
sailboarding: to go sailboarding hacer windsurf
  [ath**air**...]
sailor un marinero [maree-n**eh**-ro]
  (sport) un mar**i**no
sala de espera waiting room
salad una ensal**a**da
salami el salchich**ó**n
saldos sales
sale: is it for sale? ¿se vende? [seh b**e**ndeh]
salida exit; departure
salidas departures
salmon el salm**ó**n [sal-m**o**n]
salt la sal
same mismo [m**ee**zmo]
  the same again, please lo mismo otra vez, por
  fav**o**r [...beth...]
  it's all the same to me me es igual [meh es
  eeg-w**a**l]
sand la arena [ar**eh**-na]
sandals unas sandalias [-**a**l-yass]
sandwich un sanwich
  a ham/cheese sandwich un sanwich de
  jamón/de queso [...deh ʜam**o**n/k**eh**-so]

  ✈ Try **un bocadillo** – a baguette-type sandwich; a **sanwich** is made of sliced bread.

sanitary towels unas compresas [kompr**eh**sass]
satisfactory satisfactorio [-t**o**r-yo]
Saturday sábado
sauce la salsa
saucepan un cazo [k**a**h-tho]
saucer un platillo [-**ee**yo]
sauna una sauna [s**a**-oo-na]

sausage una salchicha [-ch**ee**-]

> ✈ Very different from UK sausages, except Frankfurters; try cured **chorizo** [chor**ee**tho] or **longaniza** [longan**ee**tha] (a type of fresh chorizo) or **morcilla** [morth**ee**ya] (black pudding). **Salchichón** is a cured salami type sausage.

say decir [deh-th**ee**r]
  how do you say…in Spanish? ¿cómo se dice… en español? […seh d**ee**-theh…]
  what did he say? ¿qué ha dicho? [keh ah d**ee**-cho]
scarf *(square)* un pañuelo [pan-yw**eh**-lo]
  (long) una bufanda [boof**a**nda]
scenery el paisaje [pɪ-s**a**ʜeh]
schedule el progr**a**ma
  on schedule en punto
  behind schedule con retraso [reh-tr**ah**-so]
scheduled flight un vuelo regular [bw**eh**-lo regool**a**r]
school la escuela [eskw**eh**-la]
scissors: a pair of scissors unas tijeras [tee-ʜ**eh**-rass]
scooter un vespino
Scotland Escocia [esk**o**th-ya]
Scottish escocés [eskoth**e**ss]
scream *(verb)* gritar [greet**a**r]
  (noun) un chillido [chee-y**ee**do]
screw el tornillo [torn**ee**yo]
screwdriver un destornillador [destorneeyad**o**r]
se alquila habitación room for rent
se prohibe la entrada no admission; no entry
se vende for sale
sea el mar
  by the sea junto al mar [ʜ**oo**nto…]
seafood unos mariscos [-r**ee**-]

search *(verb)* buscar [boo-]
search party una expedición de búsqueda
[espedeeth-yon deh booss-keh-da]
seasick: I get seasick me mareo [meh mareh-o]
seaside la orilla del mar [oreeya...]
  let's go to the seaside vámonos a la playa
  [...pla-ya]
season la temporada [...ahda]
  in the high/low season en la temporada alta/
  baja [...bah-ʜah]
seasoning el condimento
seat un asiento [ass-yento]
  is this somebody's seat? ¿es de alguien este
  asiento? [es deh alg-yen...]
seat belt el cinturón de seguridad [theentooron
  deh segooreeda]

✈ Wearing seat belts is compulsory for every
  passenger (babies must be in special seats
  and children under 12 in the back).

sea-urchin un erizo de mar [ereetho deh mar]
seaweed las algas
second segundo [segoondo]
  (of time) un segundo
  the second of... *(date)* el dos de...
secondhand de segunda mano [deh segoonda...]
see ver [bair]
  have you seen...? ¿has visto...? [ahss beesto]
  can I see the room? ¿puedo ver la habitación?
  [pwehdo...]
  see you! hasta luego [asta lweh-go]
  see you tonight hasta la noche
  oh, I see ah, ya comprendo
self-catering apartment un apartamento
self-service el autoservicio [owtosair-beeth-yo]
sell vender [bendair]
send enviar [embee-ar]

I want to send this to England quiero enviar esto a Inglaterra [kee-**eh**-ro...]

señoras ladies

sensitive sensible [sens**ee**bleh]

separate *(adjective)* separado [separ**ah**do]

  I'm separated estoy separado/a

separately: can we pay separately? ¿podemos pag**ar** por separado? [pod**eh**-moss... separ**ah**do]

September septiembre [setee-**e**mbreh]

serious serio [s**eh**-ree-o]

  I'm serious lo digo en serio [...d**ee**go...]

  this is serious esto es grave [...gr**ah**-beh]

  is it serious, doctor? ¿es grave, Doct**o**r?

service: is service included? ¿está incluido el servicio? [...sair-b**ee**th-yo]

services *(on motorway)* una área de servicios [**a**reh-a deh sair-b**ee**th-yoss]

servicios toilets

serviette una servilleta [sair-beey**eh**-ta]

several varios [b**ar**-yoss]

shade: in the shade a la sombra

shake sacudir [sakood**ee**r]

  to shake hands estrecharse la mano [-**ar**seh...]

✈ Men shake hands when they meet. Women only in more formal situations; *go to* **kiss**.

---

shallow poco profundo [...-f**oo**ndo]

shame: what a shame! ¡qué lástima! [keh...]

shampoo un champú [tchamp**oo**]

shandy una cerveza con limonada [thair-b**eh**-tha kon leemon**ah**da]

share *(room, table)* compartir [-t**ee**r]

shark un tiburón [teeboor**o**n]

sharp afil**a**do

(taste) ácido [**a**theedo]
(pain) agudo [-**oo**-]
shave afeitarse [afay-t**ar**seh]
shaver una máquina de afeitar [m**a**keena deh afay-t**ar**]
shaving foam la espuma de afeitar [esp**oo**ma deh afay-t**ar**]
shaving point un enchufe para la máquina de afeitar [en-ch**oo**feh…m**a**keena deh afay-t**ar**]
she ella [**eh**-ya]

> If there is no special emphasis Spanish doesn't use the word **ella**.
> **she is tired** está cans**a**da

sheet una sábana
shelf el estante [est**a**nteh]
shell *(sea-)* una concha
shellfish unos mariscos [-r**ee**-]
shelter un cobijo [kob**ee**-Ho]
  can we shelter here? ¿podemos cobijarnos aquí? [pod**eh**-moss kobee-H**a**rnoss ak**ee**]
sherry un jerez [Her**e**th]

> ✈ Most Spaniards drink dry forms of sherry such as a **fino** or **manzanilla** – if you want a medium or sweet sherry ask for the usual names like **amontillado** or **oloroso**, or at least specify you want a **jerez dulce** […d**oo**ltheh].

ship el barco
shirt una camisa [kam**ee**-sa]
shock un susto [s**oo**sto]
  I got an electric shock from the… me ha dado un *calambre* el… [meh ah d**a**hdo…kal**a**mbreh…]
shock-absorber el amortiguador [amorteegwad**or**]
shoelaces unos cordones [kor-d**o**-ness]

shoes los zapatos [thap**ah**-toss]

✈	men:				40	41	42	43	44	45
	women:	36	37	38	39	40	41			
	UK:		3	4	5	6	7	8	9 10 11	

shop la tienda [tee-**e**nda]
  I've some shopping to do tengo que hacer unas compras […keh ath**air**…]

> ✈ Shops open Mon-Fri 10am-9pm, closing for lunch 2pm-5pm. Closed Sat afternoon (except big chains and supermarkets) and Sunday. Bakers, butchers and fishmongers are closed Mondays too. General stores usually open much earlier than 10.00am.

shop assistant un dependiente [deh-pendee-**e**nteh]
  (female) una dependienta [-dee-**e**nta]
short corto
  (person) bajo [b**a**h-HO]
short cut un atajo [at**a**h-HO]
shorts los pantalones cortos [-**o**ness…]
shoulder el hombro [**o**mbro]
shout gritar [greet**a**r]
show: please show me por fav**o**r, *enséñeme* […ens**e**n-yeh-meh]
shower: with shower con ducha […d**oo**tcha]
shrimps unos camarones [-**o**ness]
shut cerrar [ther**a**r]
  they're shut está cerrado […ther**ah**do]
  when do you shut? ¿cuándo cierran? [kw**a**ndo thee-**e**ran]
  shut up! ¡a callar! [ah ka-y**a**r]
shy tímido
sick enfermo [-f**air**-]
  I feel sick estoy mareado […mareh-**ah**do]
  he's been sick ha vomit**a**do [ah…]
side el lado [l**ah**do]

by the side of the road a un lado de la carretera

side street una callejuela [ka-yeh-ʜweh-la]

sight: the sights of... los lugares de interés de... [loss loogaress deh eenteress deh]

sightseeing tour un recorrido turístico [rekoreedo tooreesteeko]

sign *(notice)* el letrero [letreh-ro]
(road) una señal [sen-yal]

signal: he didn't signal no señaló [no sen-yalo]

signature la firma [feerma]

silence el silencio [seelenth-yo]

silencer el silenciador [seelenth-yador]

silk la seda [seh-da]

silly tonto

silver la plata

similar parecido [pareh-theedo]

simple sencillo [sentheeyo]

since: since last week *desde* la semana pasada [dezdeh...]
since we arrived desde que llegamos [...keh yeh-gah-moss]
(because) como

sincere sincero [seen-theh-ro]

sing cantar

single: I'm single estoy soltero/a [-tehro]
a single to... un billete para... [...beel-yeh-teh...]

single room una habitación individual [abee-tath-yon eendee-beed-wal]

sister: my sister mi hermana [mee air-mah-na]

sit: can I sit here? ¿puedo sentarme aquí? [pwehdo sentarmeh akee]

size la talla [ta-ya]
(of shoes) el número [noomeh-ro]

ski el esquí [eskee]

skid patinar

skin la piel [pee-el]

skin-diving el buceo [boo-th**eh**-o]

skirt una falda

sky el cielo [thee-**eh**-lo]

sleep: I can't sleep no puedo dormir [no pw**eh**do
dorm**eer**]

sleeper *(rail)* el coche-cama [kotcheh-k**ah**ma]

sleeping bag un saco de dormir [...deh dorm**eer**]

sleeping pill una pastilla para dormir [past**ee**ya...
dorm**eer**]

sleeve la manga

slide *(photo)* una diapositiva [dee-aposee-t**ee**ba]

slow lento

  could you speak a little slower? ¿podría hablar
  un poco más despacio? [podr**ee**-a abl**ar** oon
  p**o**ko mass desp**ath**-yo]

slowly lentamente [lenta-m**en**teh]

small pequeño [pek**eh**n-yo]

  smaller notes unos billetes de menos valor
  [beey**eh**-tess deh m**eh**noss bal**or**]

small change la calderilla [kalder**ee**ya]

smell: there's a funny smell hay un *olor* raro
  [I...]

  it smells huele mal [w**eh**-leh...]

smile *(verb)* sonreír [son-reh-**eer**]

smoke el humo [**oo**mo]

  do you smoke? ¿fumas? [f**oo**mass]

  can I smoke? ¿puedo fumar? [pw**eh**do foom**ar**]

✈ Smoking is prohibited in all public buildings
(although people tend to 'forget' this), on
public transport and in cinemas. Tobacco
is still very cheap, especially if you buy it in
an **estanco** (tobacconist); very rude not to
offer to others you are with.

snack: can we just have a snack? queríamos
tom**ar** sólo una comida ligera [ker**ee**-ah-moss...
kom**ee**da lee-н**eh**-ra]

✈ Try typical Spanish **tapas** (free with alcoholic drinks in some areas) or larger **raciones** [rath-y**o**ness] if you're hungrier.

snake una serpiente [sair-pee-**e**nteh]
snorkel un respirad**o**r
snow la nieve [nee-**e**h-beh]
so: it's so hot today hace *tanto* cal**o**r hoy [**a**theh…]
  not so much no tanto
  so do I/so am I yo también […tamb-y**e**n]
soap el jabón [H**a**b**o**n]
soap powder el jabón en polvo [H**a**b**o**n…]
sober sobrio [s**o**-bree-o]
socks unos calcetines [kal-theh-t**ee**ness]
soda (water) un agua de seltz [**ah**-gwa deh selts]
soft drink una bebida no alcohólica [beb**ee**da no alko-**o**leeka]
sole la suela [sw**e**h-la]
some: some people algunas personas [alg**oo**nass pair-s**o**nass]
  can I have some grapes/some bread? ¿me pone unas uvas/un poco de pan? [meh p**o**-neh **oo**nas **oo**bass…]
  can I have some? *(of that)* quiero un poco de éso [kee-**e**h-ro…]
  (of those) quiero un poco de ésos
somebody alguien [**a**lg-yen]
something algo
sometimes algunas veces [alg**oo**nass b**e**h-thess]
somewhere en algún sitio [alg**oo**n s**ee**t-yo]
son: my son mi hijo [mee **ee**-Ho]
song una canción [kanth-y**o**n]
soon pronto
  as soon as possible lo antes posible […**a**ntess pos**ee**bleh]
  sooner antes

sore: it's sore me duele [meh dw**eh**-leh]
sore throat un dolor de garg**a**nta
sorry: (I'm) sorry ¡perdón! [pair-d**on**]
  sorry? ¿cómo?
sort: what sort of…? ¿qué tipo de…? [keh t**ee**po
  deh]
  this sort este tipo [**e**steh…]
  will you sort it out? ¿lo puede arregl**a**r? [lo
  pw**eh**deh…]
so-so así, así [as**ee**…]
sótano basement
soup la sopa
sour agrio [**a**h-gree-o]
south el sur [soor]
South Africa Sudáfrica [sood-]
souvenir un recuerdo [rekw**air**do]
spade una pala
Spain España [esp**a**n-ya]
Spaniard un español [espan-y**ol**]
  (woman) una española [espan-y**o**la]
Spanish español [espan-y**ol**]
  the Spanish los españoles [espan-y**o**-less]
spanner una llave inglesa [y**ah**-beh eengl**eh**-sa]
spare part una pieza de repuesto [pee-**eh**-tha deh
  repw**e**sto]
spare wheel la rueda de recambio [rw**eh**-da deh
  rek**a**mb-yo]
spark plug una bujía [boo-н**ee**-a]
speak hablar [abl**a**r]
  do you speak English? ¿habla inglés? [**a**bla
  eengl**e**ss]
  I don't speak Spanish no hablo español [no
  ablo espan-y**ol**]
special especial [espeth-y**a**l]
specialist un/una especialista [espeth-yal**ee**sta]
spectacles unas gafas
speed la velocidad [beloth**ee**d**a**]

he was speeding iba con excesso de velocidad [**ee**ba kon esth**eh**-so...]
speed limit el límite de velocidad [**lee**meeteh deh belotheed**a**]

✈ In towns – 50km/h (31mph); on country roads – 90km/h (56mph); on dual carriage-ways – 100km/h (62mph); on motorways – 120km/h (75mph).

speedometer el velocímetro [veh-loth**ee**-metro]
spend *(money)* gast**a**r
spice una especia [esp**e**th-ya]
   is it spicy? ¿es picante? [...peek**a**nteh]
spider una araña [ar**a**n-ya]
spoon una cuchara [kootch**a**ra]
sprain: I've sprained my... me he torcido el... [meh eh torth**ee**edo...]
spring *(of car, seat)* un muelle [mw**eh**-yeh]
   (season) la primavera [preema-b**eh**-ra]
square *(in town)* la plaza [pl**ah**-tha]
   two square metres dos metros cuadrados [...kwadr**ah**-doss]
stairs la escalera [eskal**eh**ra]
stalls las butacas de patio [boot**ah**-kass deh p**a**t-yo]
stamp un sello [s**eh**-yo]
   two stamps for England dos sellos para Inglaterra

✈ Stamps can be bought at **estancos** (tobac-conists) – look for the red and yellow stripes around the entrance – or at a post office **Correos**. Always say the destination to make sure you get the right price.

stand *(at fair)* un stand
stand-by: to fly stand-by vol**a**r con billete stand-by [...beey**eh**-teh...]

star la estrella [estr**eh**-ya]
starboard estrib**o**r
start: when does it start? ¿cuándo empieza?
 [kw**a**ndo empee-**eh**-tha]
 my car won't start mi coche no arranca [mee
 k**o**tcheh no…]
starter (of car) el mot**o**r de arranque […deh
 ar**a**nkeh]
 (food) un entremés [entreh-m**e**ss]
starving: I'm starving estoy muerto de hambre
 […mw**ai**rto deh **a**mbreh]
station la estación [estath-y**o**n]
statue una estatua [est**a**t-wa]
stay: we enjoyed our stay hemos disfrutado
 mucho de nuestra *estancia* [**eh**-moss
 deesfroot**ah**do m**oo**tcho deh nw**e**stra est**a**nth-
 ya]
 stay there quédese ahí [k**eh**-deh-seh ah-**ee**]
 I'm staying at… estoy en…
steak un filete [feel**eh**-teh]

> *YOU MAY HEAR*
> ¿muy hecho? *well done?*
> ¿normal? *medium?*
> ¿poco hecho? *rare?*

steal: my wallet's been stolen me han *robado* la
 cartera [meh an rob**ah**do…]

> ✈ You will have to go to the police **comisaría**
> to fill in a form; you'll be given a copy
> (which insurance companies will want to
> see); you will need your passport as iden-
> tity.

steep empin**a**do
steering la dirección [deerekth-y**o**n]
steering wheel el volante [bol**a**nteh]
step (of stairs) el escalón

sterling libras esterlinas [leebrass estair-leenass]
stewardess la azafata [athafahta]
sticking plaster una tirita [teereeta]
sticky pegajoso [-Hoso]
stiff duro [dooro]
still: keep still estáte quieto [esta-teh kee-ehto]
   I'm still here *todavía* estoy aquí [todabee-a estoy akee]
   I'm still waiting todavía estoy esperando
sting: I've been stung by a jelly fish me ha picado una medusa [meh ah peekahdo oona medoosa]
stink un mal olor
   it stinks huele mal [weh-leh...]
stomach el estómago
   have you got something for an upset stomach? ¿tiene algo para las molestias de estómago? [tee-eh-neh...]
stomach-ache: I have a stomach-ache me duele el vientre [meh dweh-leh el bee-entreh]
stone una piedra [pee-eh-dra]

✈ **1 stone = 6.35 kilos**

stop *(for bus)* la parada [parah-da]
   stop! ¡deténgase! [deh-tenga-seh]
   do you stop near...? ¿para cerca de...? [...thairka deh]
   could you stop here? ¿puede parar aquí? [pwehdeh...akee]
stop-over una escala
storm una tormenta
straight derecho
   go straight on siga derecho [seega...]
   a straight whisky un whisky solo
straightaway en seguida [en seh-geeda]
strange *(odd)* extraño [estran-yo]
   (unknown) desconocido [-theedo]

stranger un desconocido [-th**ee**do]
(woman) una desconocida
I'm a stranger here soy forastero/a aquí […
ak**ee**]
strawberry una fresa [fr**eh**-sa]
street la calle [k**a**-yeh]
street map un mapa de la ciudad […thee-oo-
da]
string: have you got any string? ¿tiene cuerda?
[tee-**eh**-neh kw**air**da]
stroke: he's had a stroke le ha dado un *ataque*
[…at**a**keh]
strong fuerte [fw**air**teh]
stuck *(drawer, door etc)* atascado [ataska**h**do]
student un/una estudiante [estood-y**a**nteh]
stupid estúpido [-t**oo**-]
such: such a lot tanto
suddenly de repente [deh reh-p**e**nteh]
sugar el azúcar [ath**oo**kar]
suit *(to wear)* un traje [tr**a**н-нeh]
suitable adecuado [adekw**a**нdo]
suitcase una maleta [-l**eh**-]
summer el verano [ber**a**н-no]
sun el sol
 in the sun al sol
 out of the sun a la sombra
sunbathe tom**a**r el sol
sun block una crema protect**o**ra [kr**eh**-ma…]
sunburn una quemadura sol**a**r [keh-mad**oo**ra…]
sun cream una crema sol**a**r [kr**eh**-ma…]
Sunday dom**i**ngo
sunglasses unas gafas de sol
sun lounger una tumbona [toomb**o**na]
sunstroke una insolación [-ath-yon]
suntan el bronceado [bronteh-**ah**do]
suntan oil un bronceador [bronteh-ad**o**r]
supermarket el supermercado [-mair-k**ah**do]

> ✈ Nowhere near as big as UK supermarkets
> (unless you go to a **hipermercado**) and
> don't expect to find many ready-made
> meals, prepacked vegetables etc.

supper la cena [th**eh**-na]

> ✈ Normally available 9-12pm.

sure: I'm not sure no estoy seguro/a
  [seg**oo**ro]
   are you sure? ¿está usted seguro/a? [...
   oost**eh**...]
   sure! ¡claro que sí! [kl**ah**-ro keh see]
surfboard una tabla de surf
surfing: to go surfing hacer surf [ath**air**...]
surname el apellido [apeh-y**ee**do]
swearword un taco
sweat *(verb)* sudar [sood**ar**]
sweater un jersey [н**air**-s**ay**]
sweet *(dessert)* un postre [p**o**streh]
   (wine) dulce [d**oo**ltheh]
   it's too sweet es demasiado dulce [demass-
   y**ah**do d**oo**ltheh]
sweets unos caramelos [-m**eh**-]
swerve: I had to swerve tuve que
   torcer bruscamente [t**oo**beh keh torth**air**
   brooskam**e**nteh]
swim: I'm going for a swim voy a bañarme
   [boy ah ban-y**ar**meh]
   I can't swim no sé nad**ar** [...seh...]
   let's go for a swim vamos a bañarnos [b**ah**-
   moss ah ban-y**ar**noss]
swimming costume el traje de baño [tr**ah**-нeh
   deh b**a**n-yo]
swimming pool la piscina [peess-th**ee**na]
switch el interruptor [-r**oo**pt**or**]
   to switch on encender [enthend**air**]

to **switch off** apag**a**r
Switzerland Suiza [sw**ee**tha]

T [teh]

table una mesa [m**eh**-sa]
  a table for four una mesa para cuatro personas
  [...pair-s**o**nass]
table wine un vino de mesa [...deh m**eh**-sa]
take coger [кон**a**ir]
  can I take this (with me) ? ¿puedo llevarme
  esto? [pw**eh**-do yeh-b**a**r-meh...]
  will you take me to the airport? ¿quiere
  llevarme al aeropuerto? [kee-**eh**-reh...ah-airo-
  pw**air**to]
  how long will it take? ¿cuánto tiempo tardará?
  [kw**a**nto tee-**e**mpo...]
  somebody has taken my bags se han llevado
  mis maletas [seh an yeh-b**ah**do meess...]
  can I take you out tonight? ¿quieres salir
  conmigo esta noche? [kee-**eh**-ress sal**ee**r
  konm**ee**go **e**sta n**o**tcheh]
  is this seat taken? ¿está ocupado este asiento?
  [...ass-y**e**nto]
  I'll take it lo compro
talk (verb) hablar [abl**a**r]
tall alto
tampons unos tampones [-**o**ness]
tan un bronceado [bronteh-**ah**do]
  I want to get a tan quiero broncearme [kee-**eh**-
  ro bronteh-**a**rmeh]
tank (of car) el depósito [deh-p**o**seeto]
tap el grifo [gr**ee**fo]
tape (cassette) una cinta [th**ee**nta]
tape-recorder un magnetofón
taquilla ticket office
tariff la tarifa [-r**ee**-]

taste el sabor [sa-bor]
   (in clothes etc) el gusto [goosto]
   can I taste it? ¿puedo probarlo? [pwehdo...]
taxi un taxi
   will you get me a taxi? ¿quiere buscarme un taxi? [kee-eh-reh booskarmeh...]
   where can I get a taxi? ¿dónde puedo coger un taxi? [dondeh pwehdo koнair]

> ✈ Always use official taxis (usually white with a single coloured diagonal stripe), available when the green roof light is on. You can hail them in the street, go to a rank or phone.

taxi-driver el/la taxista [-eesta]
tea té [teh]
   could I have a cup of tea? ¿me pone un té, por favor? [meh poneh...]
   could I have a pot of tea? ¿me pone un té en tetera? [...teteh-ra]

> *YOU MAY THEN HEAR*
> ¿con leche/limón? *with milk/lemon?*

teach: could you teach me some Spanish? ¿podría enseñarme un poco de español? [podree-a ensen-yarmeh...espan-yol]
teacher el profesor
   (woman) la profesora
telephone el teléfono [telefono]
   go to **phone**
telephone directory la guía telefónica [gee-a telefoneeka]
television la televisión [telebees-yon]
   I'd like to watch television quisiera ver la televisión [keess-yeh-ra bair...]
tell: could you tell me where...? ¿podría decirme dónde...? [podree-a deh-theer-meh

dondeh]

could you tell him…? ¿podría decirle…?
[…deh-theerleh]

I told him that… le dije que… [leh deeнeh keh]

temperature *(weather etc)* la temperatura [-toora]

he's got a temperature tiene fiebre [tee-**eh**-neh
fee-**eh**-breh]

tennis el tenis [**teh**-neess]

tennis ball una pelota de tenis [pelota deh t**eh**-
neess]

tennis court una pista de tenis [p**ee**sta deh t**eh**-
neess]

tennis racket una raqueta de tenis [rak**eh**-ta deh
t**eh**-neess]

tent la tienda de campaña [tee-**e**nda deh kampan-
ya]

terminus la estación terminal [estath-y**o**n
tairmeen**a**l]

terrible terrible [ter**ee**bleh]

terrific fabuloso [-bool**o**so]

text: I'll text you te mandaré un mensaje [teh
mandar**e**h oon mensa**н**eh]

text message un mensaje (de texto)
[mensa**н**eh…]

than que [keh]

bigger than… más grande que…

thanks, thank you gracias [gr**a**th-yass]

thank you very much muchas gracias
[m**oo**tchass…]

no thank you no gracias

thank you for your help gracias por su ayuda

YOU MAY THEN HEAR
de nada *you're welcome*

---

that: that man/that table ese hombre/esa mesa
[**e**h-seh **o**mbreh/**e**h-sa m**eh**-sa]

I would like that one quiero ése [kee-**eh**-ro…]

how do you pronounce that? ¿cómo se dice eso? [...seh d**ee**theh **eh**-so]
　and that? ¿y eso? [ee...]
　I think that... creo que... [kr**eh**-o keh]
the (*singular*) el/la
　(*plural*) los/las

> El/los and la/las (for 'the') correspond to un and una (for 'a') and unos and unas (for 'some').

theatre el teatro [teh-**ah**-tro]
their su [soo]

> No feminine ending; plural is **sus**. Since **su** can also mean 'his', 'her' and 'your' you can specify with **de ellos/de ellas**:
> 　**not in** *their* **car** no en el coche de ellos/ ellas

theirs: It's theirs es (el) suyo/(la) suya
　[...s**oo**yo...]
them (*objects*) los; las
　(*persons*) les [less]
　I've lost them los/las he perdido [loss/lass eh pair-d**ee**do]
　I sent it to them se lo envié (a ellos/ellas) [se lo emb**ee**-eh (ah **eh**-yoss/**eh**-yass)]
　for/with them para/con ellos/ellas
　who? – them ¿quiénes? – ellos/ellas
then entonces [ent**o**n-thess]
there allí [ah-y**ee**]
　how do I get there? ¿cómo se llega? [...seh y**eh**-ga]
　is there/are there...? ¿hay...? [ɪ]
　there isn't/there aren't... no hay...
　there you are (*giving something*) tome [t**o**hmeh]
these estos/estas
they ellos/ellas [**eh**-yoss/**eh**-yass]

> If there is no special emphasis Spanish
> doesn't use the word **ellos** or **ellas**.
> **where are they?** ¿dónde están?

thick grueso [grw**eh**-so]
  (stupid) estúpido [-t**oo**-]
thief un ladrón
thigh el muslo [m**oo**zlo]
thin delg**a**do
thing una cosa
  I've lost all my things he perdido todas mis
  cosas [eh paird**ee**do...]
think pens**a**r
  I'll think it over lo pensaré [...pensar**eh**]
  I think so creo que sí [kr**eh**-o keh see]
  I don't think so no creo
third *(adjective)* tercero [tair-th**eh**-ro]
thirsty: I'm thirsty tengo sed [...seth]
this este/esta [**e**steh...]
  can I have this one? ¿me da éste?
  this is my wife/this is Mr... ésta es mi mujer/
  éste es el señor.... [...mee moo-н**air**...]
  this is very good esto está muy bien [...mwee
  bee-**e**n]
  this is... *(on telephone)* soy...
  is this...? ¿es esto...?
those esos/esas [**eh**-soss...]
  no, not these, those! ¡éstos no, ésos!
  how much are those? ¿cuánto valen ésos?
  [kw**a**nto b**a**h-len...]
thread el hilo [**ee**lo]
throat la garg**a**nta
throttle *(of motorbike, boat)* el acelerador [atheh-
  leh-rad**o**r]
through *(across)* a través de [ah trab**e**ss deh]
throw tirar [teer**a**r]
thumb el dedo pulgar [d**eh**do poolg**a**r]

thunder el trueno [troo-**eh**-no]
thunderstorm una tormenta
Thursday jueves [Hw**eh**-bess]
ticket un billete [beey**eh**-teh]
   (cinema) una entrada [entr**ah**da]
   (cloakroom etc) un ticket [t**ee**keh]

✈ *go to* **bus, train, metro.**

tie *(necktie)* una corb**a**ta
tight *(clothes)* ajustado [aHoost**ah**do]
tights unos leotardos [leh-o-t**a**rdoss]
time el tiempo [tee-**e**mpo]
   I haven't got time no tengo tiempo
   for the time being por el momento
   this time esta vez […beth]
   next time la próxima vez
   three times tres veces [tress b**e**thess]
   have a good time! ¡que te diviertas! [keh teh
   deeb-y**ai**rtass]
   what's the time? ¿qué hora es? [keh **o**ra ess]

✈ 24hr system is used. Remember to add one
   hour to British time when you arrive.

HOW TO TELL THE TIME
it's one o'clock es la una […**oo**na]
it's two/three/four o'clock son las dos/
tres/cuatro […doss/tress/kw**a**tro]
it's 5/10/20/25 past seven son las
siete y cinco/diez/veinte/veinticinco
[…ee th**ee**nko/dee-**e**th/b**ay**nteh/bayntee-
th**ee**nko]
it's quarter past eight/eight fifteen son
las ocho y cuarto […ee kw**a**rto]
it's half past nine/nine thirty son las
nueve y media […nw**e**h-beh ee m**eh**d-ya]
it's 25/20/10/5 to ten son las diez menos

> veinticinco/veinte/diez/cinco [...meh-
> noss...]
> **it's quarter to eleven/10.45** son las once
> menos cuarto
> **it's twelve o'clock (am/pm)** son las doce
> (de la mañana/de la noche) [...dotheh deh
> la man-yah-na/deh la notcheh]
> **at one o'clock** a la una [ah...]
> **at three thirty** a las tres y media

timetable el horario [or-ar-yo]
tin *(can)* una lata
tin-opener un abrelatas [ah-breh-lah-tass]
tip una propina [-pee-]
  is the tip included? ¿va incluída la propina? [ba
  eenkloo-eeda...]

> ✈ Tip the same people as in the UK, although
>   Spaniards tend not to be that generous.

tirar pull
tired cansado
  I'm tired estoy cansado/a
tissues unos kleenex
to: to Cadiz/England a Cádiz/Inglaterra [ah...]
  to Juan's a casa de Juan [...Hwan]
  go to time
toast *(piece of)* una tostada
tobacco el tabaco
today hoy [oy]
toe el dedo del pie [dehdo del pee-eh]
together junto [Hoonto]
  we're together venimos juntos [beneemoss...]
  can we pay all together? ¿puede cobrarlo
  todo junto? [pwehdeh...]
toilet los aseos [ass-eh-oss]
  where are the toilets? ¿dónde están los aseos?
  [dondeh...]

I have to go to the toilet tengo que ir al wáter
[...keh eer al b*ah*-tair]

✈ Not many public conveniences; usually in stations; don't hesitate to go into a bar or café and use their toilet; that's normal, but remember to ask for permission if you are not a customer.

can I use your toilet? ¿puedo utilizar el cuarto de baño? [pw*eh*do ooteeleeth*a*r el kw*a*rto deh b*a*n-yo]

toilet paper: there's no toilet paper no hay papel higiénico [no ɪ pap*e*l eeн-y*eh*-neeko]

tomato un tomate [tom*ah*-teh]

tomato juice un zumo de tomate [th*oo*-mo deh tom*ah*-teh]

tomato ketchup el catsup [kat-s*oo*p]

tomorrow mañana [man-y*ah*-na]
  tomorrow morning mañana por la mañana
  tomorrow afternoon mañana por la tarde [...t*a*rdeh]
  tomorrow evening mañana por la tarde
  (later) mañana por la noche [...n*o*tcheh]
  the day after tomorrow pasado mañana
  see you tomorrow hasta mañana [*a*sta...]

tongue la lengua [l*e*ng-gwa]

tonic (water) una tónica

tonight esta noche [...n*o*tcheh]

tonsillitis la amigdalitis [-*ee*teess]

too demasiado [demass-y*ah*do]
  (also) también [tamb-y*e*n]
  that's too much eso es demasiado
  me too yo también

tool una herramienta [eram-y*e*nta]

tooth un diente [dee-*e*nteh]
  (back tooth) la muela [mw*eh*-la]

toothache: I've got toothache tengo dol*o*r de

muelas [...deh mw**eh**-lass]

toothbrush un cepillo de dientes [thep**ee**yo deh dee-**e**ntess]

toothpaste la pasta dentífrica [...dent**ee**freeka]

top: on top of encima de [enth**ee**ma deh]

  on the top floor en el último piso [...p**ee**-so]

  at the top en lo alto

torch una linterna [leent**air**na]

total el total [tot**a**l]

tough duro [d**oo**ro]

tour un viaje [bee-**ah**-Heh]

  (of town) un recorrido [reh-korr**ee**do]

  (of museum, gallery) una visita

  we'd like to go on a tour of... nos gustaría hacer un viaje por... [noss goostar**ee**-a ath**air**...]

  we're touring around estamos de turismo [...toor**ee**zmo]

tourist un/una turista [toor**ee**sta]

tourist office la oficina de turismo [ofeeth**ee**na deh toor**ee**zmo]

tow *(verb)* remolcar

  can you give me a tow? ¿puede remolcarme? [pw**eh**deh...]

towards hacia [**a**th-ya]

  he was coming straight towards me venía derecho hacia mí [ben**ee**-a der**eh**-cho **a**th-ya mee]

towel una toalla [to-**ay**-ya]

town una ciudad [thee-ood**a**]

  (smaller) un pueblo [pw**eh**-blo]

  in town en el centro [...th**e**ntro]

  would you take me into town? ¿podría llevarme al centro? [podr**ee**-a yeh-b**a**r-meh...]

towrope un cable de remolque [k**a**h-bleh deh rem**o**lkeh]

traditional tradicional [tradeeth-yon**a**l]

  a traditional Spanish meal una comida

española tradicional [...kom**ee**da espan-y**o**la...]
traffic el tráfico
traffic jam un atasco
traffic lights los semáforos

> ✈ Often suspended above junctions; they go straight from red to green (no red-amber warning).

train el tren

> ✈ Best to book in advance as trains tend to be busy; train travel is slow unless you get the new high speed AVE between Madrid-Seville, Madrid-Lérida or Madrid-Barcelona.

trainers las zapatillas de deporte [thapat**ee**yass deh deh-p**o**rteh]
train station la estación [estath-y**o**n]
tranquillizers unos calmantes [-m**a**ntess]
translate traducir [-ooth**ee**r]
  would you translate that for me? ¿quiere traducirme eso, por favor? [kee-**eh**-reh tradooth**ee**r-meh...]
travel viajar [bee-a**н**ar]
travel agent's una agencia de viajes [a**н**enth-ya deh bee-**ah**-нess]
traveller's cheque un cheque de viaje [ch**eh**-keh deh bee-**ah**-нeh]
tree un árbol
tremendous (very good) fenomenal
trim: just a trim, please recórtemelo nada más [reh-k**o**rteh-meh-lo...]
trip (journey) un viaje [bee-a**н**eh]
  (outing) una excursión [eskoors-y**o**n]
  we want to go on a trip to... queremos hacer una excursión a... [ker**eh**-moss ath**air**...]
trouble unos problemas [probl**eh**-mass]
  I'm having trouble with... estoy teniendo

problemas con… […ten-y**e**ndo…]
trousers los pantalones [-l**o**-ness]
true verdadero [bair-dad**eh**-ro]
  it's not true no es verdad […bair-d**a**]
trunks *(swimming)* el bañador [ban-ya-d**o**r]
try intent**a**r
  can I try it on? ¿puedo probármelo? [pw**eh**do
  pro-b**a**r-meh-lo]
T-shirt una camiseta [kamee-s**eh**-ta]
Tuesday martes [m**a**rtess]
tunnel un túnel [t**oo**nel]
turn: where do we turn off? ¿dónde tenemos
  que desviarnos? [d**o**ndeh ten-**eh**-moss keh dess-
  bee-**a**rnoss]
twice dos veces […b**e**thess]
  twice as much el doble […d**o**bleh]
twin beds dos camas […k**a**mass]
twin room una habitación con dos camas [abee-
  tath-y**o**n…k**a**mass]
typical típico [t**ee**-]
tyre un neumático [neh-oom**a**tiko]
  I need a new tyre necesito un neumático
  nuevo [nethess**ee**to … nw**eh**-bo]

 tyre pressure

lb/sq in	18	20	22	26	28	30
kg/sq cm	1.3	1.4	1.5	1.7	2	2.1

U [oo]

ugly feo [f**eh**-o]
ulcer una úlcera [**oo**l-theh-ra]
umbrella un paraguas [par**ah**g-wass]
uncle: my uncle mi tío [mee t**ee**-o]
uncomfortable incómodo
unconscious inconsciente [eenkons-thee-**e**nteh]
under debajo de [deb**ah**-нo deh]

underdone poco hecho [...etcho]

underground *(rail)* el metro

understand: I understand lo entiendo [lo ent-yendo]

  I don't understand no entiendo

  do you understand? ¿entiende? [ent-yendeh]

undo deshacer [dess-athair]

unfriendly antipático [antee-pateeko]

unhappy desgraciado [dess-grath-yahdo]

United States los Estados Unidos [estah-doss ooneedoss]

university la universidad [oonee-bairseeda]

unleaded la gasolina sin plomo [...seen...]

unlock abrir [abreer]

until hasta que [asta keh]

  until next year hasta el año que viene [asta el an-yo keh bee-eh-neh]

unusual poco corriente [...kor-yenteh]

up arriba [areeba]

  he's not up yet todavía no se ha levantado [todabee-a no seh ah...]

  what's up? ¿qué pasa? [keh...]

  up there allí arriba [ah-yee...]

upside-down al revés [al reh-bess]

upstairs arriba [areeba]

urgent urgente [oor-Henteh]

us nos [noss]

  can you help us? ¿nos puede ayudar? [...pwehdeh...]

  with/for us con/para nosotros [...nossotross] *(female)* con/para nosotras

  who? – us ¿quién? – nosotros/nosotras

USA EE.UU.

> This Spanish abbreviation is a written form only. In speaking you say **los Estados Unidos**.

use: can I use…? ¿puedo usar…? [pweh-do oosar]
useful útil [ooteel]
usual habitual [abeet-wal]
  as usual como de costumbre […deh kostoom-breh]
usually normalmente [nor-mal-menteh]
U-turn un viraje en U [beerah-Heh en oo]

V [oo-veh]

vacate *(room)* desocupar [-koo-]
vacation las vacaciones [bakath-yoness]
vaccination una vacuna [-koo-]
vacuum flask un termo [tairmo]
valid válido [baleedo]
  how long is it valid for? ¿hasta cuándo es valido? [asta kwando…]
valley el valle [ba-yeh]
valuable valioso [balee-oso]
  will you look after my valuables? ¿quiere cuidar de mis objetos de valor? [kee-eh-reh kweedar deh meess ob-Heh-toss deh balor]
value el valor [balor]
van una furgoneta [foorgoneh-ta]
vanilla vainilla [bɪ-neeya]
Vd., Vds. = usted, ustedes you
veal la ternera [tair-neh-ra]
vegetables las verduras [bair-doorass]
vegetarian vegetariano [beh-Hetaree-ah-no]

> ✈ It's not common for restaurants to offer veggie-friendly menus; better to go to specialist vegetarian restaurants.

velocidad limitada speed limit
venta de sellos stamps
ventilator el ventilador [benteela-dor]
very muy [mwee]

very much mucho [**moo**tcho]
via por
village un pueblo [p**weh**-blo]
vine una vid [b**ee**th]
vinegar el vinagre [been**ah**-greh]
vineyard un viñedo [been-y**eh**-do]
violent violento [bee-o-l**e**nto]
visit *(verb)* visitar [beesee**ta**r]
vodka un vodka
voice la voz [voth]
voltage el voltaje [bolt**ah**-Heh]

✈ 220 as in the UK.

W [**oo**-veh d**o**-bleh]

waist la cintura [theent**oo**ra]
wait: will we have to wait long? ¿tendremos
  que *esperar* mucho? [tendr**eh**-moss keh espeh-r**a**r
  m**oo**tcho]
  wait for me espérame [esp**eh**-ra-meh]
  I'm waiting for a friend/my wife estoy
  esperando a un amigo/a mi mujer […mee moo-
  н**ai**r]
waiter un camarero [-r**eh**-ro]
  waiter! ¡camarero!
waitress la camarera [kamar**eh**-ra]
wake: will you wake me up at 7.30? ¿quiere
  despertarme a las siete y media? [kee-**eh**-reh
  despair-t**a**rmeh ah lass see-**eh**-teh ee m**eh**d-ya]
Wales Gales [g**ah**-less]
walk: can we walk there? ¿se puede *ir a pie*?
  [seh pw**eh**deh eer ah pee-**eh**]
walking shoes los zapatos de campo [thap**ah**-
  toss…]
wall el muro
  (inside) la pared [par**eh**]

wallet la cartera [kart**eh**-ra]
want: I want... quiero... [kee-**eh**-ro]
  I want to talk to... quiero hablar con... [... abl**a**r...]
  what do you want? ¿qué quiere usted? [keh kee-**eh**-reh oost**eh**]
  I don't want to no quiero
  he/she wants to... quiere...
war la guerra [g**era**]
warm caliente [kal-y**e**nteh]
warning un aviso [ab**ee**so]
was

> There are two Spanish verbs for 'to be': **ser** and **estar** (more at **be**).
>
> **I was** era [**eh**-ra]
> **you were** *(familiar)* eras
> **you were** *(polite)* era
> **he/she/it was** era
> **we were** éramos
> **you were** *(familiar plural)* érais [**eh**-rɪs]
> **you were** *(polite plural)* eran
> **they were** eran
>
> **I was** estaba
> **you were** *(familiar)* estabas
> **you were** *(polite)* estaba
> **he/she/it was** estaba
> **we were** estábamos
> **you were** *(familiar plural)* estábais [est**ah**-bɪs]
> **you were** *(polite plural)* estaban
> **they were** estaban

wash: can you wash these for me? ¿podría lavármelos? [podr**ee**-a lab**a**r-meh-loss]
washbasin un lavabo [lab**ah**bo]
washer *(for nut)* una arandela [-d**eh**la]
washing machine una lavad**o**ra

washing powder el jabón en polvo [Hab**o**n...]
wasp una avispa [-b**ee**-]
watch *(wristwatch)* el reloj [reh-l**o**H]
   will you watch my bags for me? ¿me podría
   vigilar las maletas? [meh podr**ee**-a beeH**ee**l**a**r...]
   watch out! ¡cuidado! [kweed**ah**do]
water el agua [**ah**g-wa]
   can I have some water? ¿puede traerme agua?
   [pw**eh**deh trah-**air**meh...]
   hot and cold running water agua caliente y
   fría [...kal-y**e**nteh ee fr**ee**-a]

> ✈ Tap water is perfectly safe to drink in practi-
> cally all the country, although sometimes
> heavily chlorinated; ask the locals if it's bet-
> ter to drink bottled water.

waterproof impermeable [eempair-meh-**ah**-
   bleh]
waterskiing el esquí acuático [esk**ee** akw**a**teeko]
way: it's this way es por aquí [...ak**ee**]
   it's that way es por ahí [...ah-**ee**]
   do it this way hazlo así [**a**thlo as**ee**]
   no way! ¡de ninguna manera! [deh neen-g**oo**na
   man**eh**ra]
   is it on the way to...? ¿queda en el camino
   a...? [k**eh**da...kam**ee**no...]
   could you tell me the way to get to...?
   ¿podría indic**a**rme el camino para...? [podr**ee**-
   a...]
   go to **where** *for answers*
we nosotros/nosotras [noss**o**tross...]

If there is no special emphasis Spanish
doesn't use the word **nosotros** or (if it's
women speaking) **nosotras**.
   we're English somos ingleses/inglesas
   [...eengl**eh**-sess...]

weak *(person)* débil [d**eh**-beel]
weather el tiempo [tee-**e**mpo]
  what filthy weather! ¡qué tiempo tan
  asqueroso! [keh tee-**e**mpo tan askeh-r**o**so]
  what's the weather forecast? ¿cuál es el
  pronóstico del tiempo? [kwal ess...]

> *YOU MAY THEN HEAR*
> va a hacer sol *it'll be sunny*
> va a llover *it's going to rain*
> va a mejorar el tiempo *the weather's going
> to improve*

website un sitio web [s**ee**t-yo...]
Wednesday miércoles [mee-**air**-koless]
week una semana [sem**ah**na]
  a week today de hoy en una semana [deh
  oy...]
  a week tomorrow de mañana en una semana
weekend: at the weekend el fin de semana [el
  feen deh sem**ah**na]
weight el peso [p**eh**-so]
welcome: you're welcome de nada [deh
  n**ah**da]
well: I'm not feeling well no me encuentro *bien*
  [no meh enkw**e**ntro bee-**e**n]
  he's not well no está bueno [...bw**eh**-no]
  how are you? – very well, thanks ¿cómo está
  usted? – muy bien, gracias [...oost**eh** mwee bee-
  en gr**ah**t-yass]
  you speak English very well habla inglés muy
  bien [**ah**-bla eengl**e**ss...]
  well, well! ¡vaya, vaya! [b**y**-ya]
Welsh galés [gal**e**ss]
were *go to* **was**
west el oeste [o-**e**steh]
West Indies las Antillas [ant**ee**yass]
wet mojado [moнah́do]

(weather) lluvioso [yoovee-**o**so]

wet suit un traje isotérmico [tr**ah**-Heh eesso-t**air**-meeko]

what? ¿qué? [keh]

  what is that? ¿qué es eso? [keh es **eh**-so]

  what for? ¿para qué?

  what train? ¿qué tren?

wheel la rueda [rw**eh**-da]

wheelchair una silla de inválido [s**ee**-ya deh eemb**a**leedo]

when? ¿cuándo? [kw**a**ndo]

  when is breakfast? ¿a qué hora es el desayuno? [ah keh **o**ra…]

  when we arrived cuando llegamos [kw**a**ndo yeh-g**a**moss]

where? ¿dónde? [d**o**ndeh]

  where is…? ¿dónde está…?

> *YOU MAY THEN HEAR*
> siga derecho *go straight on*
> la primera/segunda *the first/second*
> a la izquierda/derecha *on the left/right*
> siga hasta el segundo cruce *go as far as the second crossroads*
> ahí *down there*

which? ¿qué? [keh]

  which one? ¿cuál? [kwal]

> *YOU MAY THEN HEAR*
> éste/ésta *this one*
> ése/ésa *that one*
> aquél/aquélla *that one over there*

whisky un whisky

white blanco

white wine un vino blanco [b**ee**no…]

Whitsun Pentecostés

who? ¿quién? [kee-**en**]

whose: whose is this? ¿de quién es esto? [deh kee-**e**n…]

> *YOU MAY THEN HEAR*
> es mío/mía *it's mine*

why? ¿por qué? […keh]
why not? ¿por qué no?

> *YOU MAY THEN HEAR*
> porque *because*

wide ancho
wife: my wife mi mujer [mee moo-H**ai**r]
will: when will it be finished? ¿cuándo estará terminado? [kw**a**ndo estar**a**…]
  will you do it? ¿lo puede hacer? [lo pw**eh**deh ath**ai**r]
  I'll come back volveré [bol-beh-r**eh**]
win gan**a**r
  who won? ¿quién ha ganado? [kee-**e**n ah…]
wind el viento [bee-**e**nto]
window la ventana [bent**a**na]
  (of car, plane) la ventanilla [bentan**ee**ya]
  (of shop) el escaparate [-**ah**-teh]
window seat un asiento de ventanilla [ass-y**e**nto deh bentan**ee**ya]
windscreen el parabrisas [parabr**ee**-sass]
windscreen wipers los limpiaparabrisas [leemp-ya-parabr**ee**-sass]
windy: it's too windy hace demasiado viento [**a**theh demass-y**ah**do bee-**e**nto]
wine el vino [b**ee**no]
  can I see the wine list? ¿me enseña la lista de vinos? [meh ens**e**n-ya la l**ee**sta deh b**ee**-noss]
  two red wines dos vinos tintos […t**ee**ntoss]

> **a bottle of house white/red** una botella de blanco/tinto de la casa [bot**eh**-ya…]

✈ The best wines have DOC (Denominación de Origen Controlada) and the place where bottled on the label.

Red: most famous from **Rioja** or **Ribera del Duero**, but **Valdepeñas** made with Tempranillo grapes is a good cheaper alternative.

White: same regions but try **Barbadillo** from the south or **Alvarinho** from Galicia (a young slightly sparkling white).

Rosé: **Penedés** and **Vino de Aguja**.

Málaga: sweet port-style red.

Mosto: a young often homemade rough wine from the local area which is fun to try in local bars straight from the barrel.

Vino de mesa is only really used for making sangria and **tinto de verano** (red wine spritzer).

winter el invierno [eembee-**air**-no]

wire el alambre [al**a**mbreh]

(electric) el cable eléctrico [...k**ah**-bleh...]

wish: best wishes saludos [-**oo**dos]

with con

without sin [seen]

witness un/una testigo [test**ee**go]

  will you act as a witness for me? ¿quiere actuar como testigo mío? [kee-**eh**-reh ak-too-**a**r **k**omo test**ee**go m**ee**-o]

woman una mujer [moo-н**air**]

  women las mujeres [moo-н**eh**-ress]

wonderful estupendo [estoop**e**ndo]

won't: it won't start no arranca

wood la madera [mad**eh**-ra]

  (forest) el bosque [b**o**skeh]

wool la lana

word una pal**a**bra

I don't know that word no conozco esa
palabra [no kon**o**thko…]
work trabajar [trabaH**a**r]
  I work in London trabajo en Londres [trab**ah**-Ho
  en l**o**ndress]
  it's not working no funciona [foonth-y**o**na]
worry: I'm worried about him estoy
preocupado por él […preh-okoo-p**ah**do…]
  don't worry no se preocupe [no seh preh-
  ok**oo**peh]
worse: it's worse es peor […peh-**o**r]
worst el peor [peh-**o**r]
worth: it's not worth that much no vale tanto
[…b**ah**-leh…]
worthwhile: is it worthwhile going to…? ¿vale
la pena ir a…? [b**ah**-leh la p**eh**-na eer ah]
wrap: could you wrap it up? ¿me lo envuelve?
[meh lo embw**e**l-beh]
wrench *(tool)* una llave inglesa [y**ah**-beh eengl**eh**-
sa]
wrist la muñeca [moon-y**eh**-ka]
write escribir [eskreeb**ee**r]
  could you write it down? ¿puede escribírmelo?
  [pw**eh**deh eskreeb**ee**r-meh-lo]
  I'll write to you te escribiré [teh eskreebeer**eh**]
writing paper el pap**e**l de escribir […deh
eskreeb**ee**r]
wrong: I think the bill's wrong me parece que
la cuenta está *equivocada* [meh par**eh**-theh keh la
kw**e**nta est**a** eh-keebo-k**ah**-da]
  there's something wrong with… le pasa algo
  a… [leh…ah…]
  you're wrong se equivoca [seh eh-keebo-ka]
  that's the wrong key no es ésa la llave [no ess
  eh-sa…]
  sorry, wrong number *(I have)* perdone, me
  he equivocado de número [pairdo-neh…deh

n**oo**meh-ro]
(you have) se ha equivocado de número [seh
ah…]
I got the wrong train me he equivocado de
tren
what's wrong? ¿qué pasa? [keh…]

Y [eegree-**eh**-ga]

yacht un yate [y**ah**-teh]
yard

✈ 1 yard = 91.44 cms = 0.91 m

year un año [**a**n-yo]
 this year este año
 next year el año que viene […keh bee-**eh**-
 neh]
yellow amarillo [amar**ee**yo]
yellow pages las páginas amarillas [p**ah**-ʜeenass
 amar**ee**yass]
yes sí [see]
yesterday ayer [ah-y**air**]
 the day before yesterday anteayer [anteh-ah-
 y**air**]
 yesterday morning ayer por la mañana […
 man-y**ah**-na]
 yesterday afternoon ayer por la tarde […
 t**a**rdeh]
yet: is it ready yet? ¿está listo *ya*?
 not yet todavía no [todab**ee**-a…]
yoghurt un yogur [yog**oor**]
you

Which word you use depends on how
friendly you are with the person. If you are
talking to a stranger, especially someone
older, then use:

(polite) usted [oost**eh**]
(polite plural) ustedes [oost**eh**-dess]

Otherwise you can use:
(familiar singular) tú [too]
(familiar plural) vosotros/vosotras

If there is no special emphasis Spanish doesn't use any of these.
do you speak English? ¿habla inglés?
or in the familiar form
do you speak English? ¿hablas inglés?

Object forms are:
I don't understand you no *le* entiendo
[no leh ent-y**e**ndo]
(to a woman) no *la* entiendo
I'll send it to you *se* lo enviaré [seh lo embeear**eh**]
(familiar) *te* lo enviaré [teh lo embeear**eh**]

With prepositions:
for you para usted
(familiar) para ti [t**ee**]
with you con usted
(familiar) contigo [-t**ee**-]

is that you? ¿es usted?
(familiar) ¿eres tú? [**eh**ress too]
who? – you ¿quién? – usted/ustedes/tú/vosotros/vosotras

young joven [**HO**-ben]
your su [soo]

No feminine ending; plural is **sus**. Since **su** can also mean 'his', 'her' and 'their' you can specify with **de usted/ustedes**:
not in your car no en el coche de usted

> The familiar form is **tu** or **vuestro/vuestra**
> if you are talking to more than one person.
>   **are these your sunglasses?** ¿son tus
>   gafas de sol?

yours suyo/suya [sooyo...]
  (familiar) tuyo/tuya [tooyo...]
youth hostel un albergue juvenil [al-bair-geh
  Hoobeh-neel]

Z [theh-ta]

zero cero [theh-ro]
  below zero bajo cero [bah-Ho...]
zip una cremallera [kreh-ma-yeh-ra]
  could you put a new zip on? ¿podría cambiar
  la cremallera? [podree-a kambee-ar...]
zona azul restricted parking

ALGERIA

MAR MEDITERRÁNEO
(MEDITERRANEAN)

km   300

0

Baleares

Cadaqués
Gerona
Barcelona
Tarragona

Ibiza

Benidorm
Valencia
Torrevieja
Cartagena

Alicante
Murcia   Mojácar
Almería
Las Alpujarras

FRANCE
San Sebastián
Bilbao
(BASQUE COUNTRY)
PAÍS VASCO
Pamplona
ANDORRA
P i r i n e o s
CATALUÑA (CATALONIA)
Huesca
Lérida
Zaragoza
Ebro
Teruel
Cuenca
Logroño
Soria
Albacete

Santander
Cordillera Cantábrica

Oviedo

Lugo
León
Orense
GALICIA

Burgos
Palencia
Valladolid
Duero
Segovia
Ávila
Madrid
Salamanca
Zamora
Tajo (Tagus)
Cáceres
Mérida
Badajoz
Guadiana
Aranjuez
Toledo

Baeza
Guadalquivir
Córdoba
Granada
Sierra Nevada
Nerja
Carmona
Sevilla
Málaga
Marbella
Estepona
ANDALUCÍA
Jerez
Cádiz
Huelva
GIBRALTAR

La Coruña
Santiago
Pontevedra
Bayona

PORTUGAL

OCÉANO
ATLÁNTICO
(ATLANTIC
OCEAN)

FRANCE

Cadaqués
Tossa de Mar
Lloret de Mar
Santa Susanna
Barcelona
Salou
Tarragona

Costa Brava

Cap Salou

Costa Dorada

Ebro

Zaragoza

B a l e a r e s

MAR MEDITERRÁNEO
(MEDITERRANEAN)

Valencia

Alicante

Costa Blanca

Benidorm
Torrevieja
Cartagena

Madrid

Toledo

Mojácar

Almería

Costa de Almería

N
E
S
W

Granada

Córdoba

Roquetas de Mar
Nerja

Benalmádena
Torremolinos
Marbella
Málaga
Estepona

Costa del Sol

GIBRALTAR

Sevilla

150

km

0

PORTUGAL

MOROCCO

0   km   15

Fornells
Cala Morell
Playa de Fornells
Arenal d'en Castell
Cala'n Forcat
Ciutadella
Son Parc
Cala'n Blanes
Cala Blanca
Ferreries
Es Mercadal
M e n o r c a
Cala Galdana
Alaior
Mahón (Maó)
Santo Tomás
Son Bou
Airport
Villacarlos (Es Castell)
Sant Lluís
S'Algar
Binibeca
Punta Prima

Menorca
Mallorca

Puerto Pollensa
Alcúdia
Can Picafort
Valldemossa
M a l l o r c a
Palma (de Mallorca)
Cala Millor
Andratx
Palma airport
Manacor
Portals Nous
Porto Cristo
Santa Ponsa
Palma Nova
Magaluf
Arenal
Calas (de Mallorca)
Colónia de Sant Jordi

MAR MEDITERRÁNEO
(MEDITERRANEAN)

0   km   15

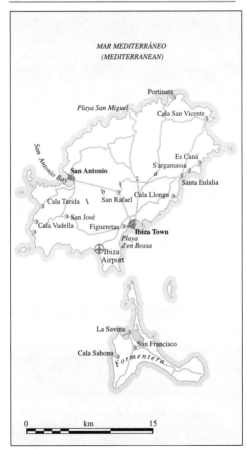

MAR MEDITERRÁNEO
(MEDITERRANEAN)

Portinatx

Playa San Miguel

Cala San Vicente

San Antonio Bay

Es Caná

San Antonio

S'argamassa

Santa Eulalia

Cala Tarida

San Rafael

Cala Llonga

Cala Vadella

San José

Cala Vadella

Figueretas

Ibiza Town

Playa d'en Bossa

Ibiza
Airport

La Savina

San Francisco

Cala Sahona

Formentera

0   km   15

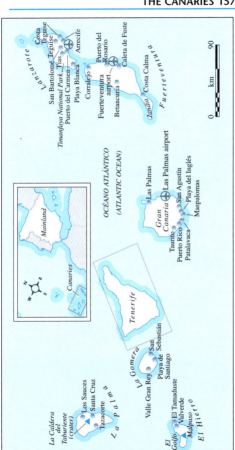

to Santa Cruz de la Palma

to Morro Jable

to Las Palmas

to Agaete

Punta del Hidalgo

Bajamar

Tegueste

La Laguna

Santa Cruz

Tenerife Norte

San Isidro

Las Caletillas

Puerto de la Cruz

La Matanza

La Orotava

Garachico

▲ Mount Teide

Granadilla

El Médano

Buenavista

Santiago

La Escalona

Adeje

Arona

Los Gigantes

Playa de la Arena

Playa Paraíso

La Caleta

Playa de las Américas

Los Cristianos

Reina Sofía

to Santa Cruz de la Palma

to San Sebastián

to Valle Gran Rey

to Valverde

N E S W

0   km   21

Numbers

0	cero	[theh-ro]
1	uno	[oono]
2	dos	[doss]
3	tres	[tress]
4	cuatro	[kwatro]
5	cinco	[theenko]
6	seis	[sayss]
7	siete	[see-eh-teh]
8	ocho	[otcho]
9	nueve	[nweh-beh]
10	diez	[dee-eth]
11	once	[on-theh]
12	doce	[dotheh]
13	trece	[treh-theh]
14	catorce	[kator-theh]
15	quince	[keen-theh]
16	dieciséis	[dee-ethee-sayss]
17	diecisiete	[dee-ethee-see-eh-teh]
18	dieciocho	[dee-ethee-otcho]
19	diecinueve	[dee-ethee-nweh-beh]
20	veinte	[bayn-teh]
21	veintiuno	
22	ventidos	
23	ventitres	
24	venticuatro	
25	venticinco	
26	ventiséis	
27	ventisiete	
28	ventiocho	
29	ventinueve	
30	treinta	[traynta]
31	treinta y uno	[traynt-ı-oono]
40	cuarenta	[kwarenta]
41	cuarenta y uno	[kwarent-ı-oono]
50	cincuenta	[theen-kwenta]

51	cincuenta y uno [theen-kwent-ɪ-**oo**no]
60	sesenta
61	sesenta y uno [sessent-ɪ-**oo**no]
70	setenta
71	setenta y uno [setent-ɪ-**oo**no]
80	ochenta
81	ochenta y uno [otchent-ɪ-**oo**no]
90	noventa
91	noventa y uno [novent-ɪ-**oo**no]
100	cien [thee-**en**]
101	ciento uno
165	ciento sesenta y cinco
200	doscientos [doss-thee-**en**toss]
300	trescientos [tress-thee-**en**toss]
400	cuatrocientos [kwatro-thee-**en**toss]
500	quinientos [keen-y**en**toss]
600	seiscientos [sayss-thee-**en**toss]
700	setecientos [seteh-thee-**en**toss]
800	ochocientos [otcho-thee-**en**toss]
900	novecientos [noveh-thee-**en**toss]
1,000	mil [meel]
2,000	dos mil
4,653	cuatro mil seiscientos cincuenta y tres
1,000,000	un millón [meel-y**on**]

NB In Spain a comma is used for a decimal point; for thousands use a full stop, eg 3.000

The alphabet: how to spell in Spanish

a [ah] **b** [beh] **c** [theh] **d** [deh] **e** [eh] **f** [ef-feh]
g [Heh] **h** [**a**tcheh] **i** [ee] **j** [Hota] **k** [ka] **l** [**eh**-leh]
m [**eh**-meh] **n** [**eh**-neh] **ñ** [en-yeh] **o** [oh]
p [peh] **q** [koo] **r** [**eh**-reh] **s** [**eh**-seh] **t** [teh]
u [oo] **v** [**oo**-veh] **w** [**oo**-veh do-bleh] **x** [**e**keess]
y [eegree-**eh**-ga] **z** [th**eh**-ta]